COLLINS WILD GUIDE

INSECTS
of Britain and Europe

Bob Gibbons

HarperCollinsPublishers

HarperCollins*Publishers*
77–85 Fulham Palace Road
London
W6 8JB

00 02 04 03 01 99

2 4 6 8 10 9 7 5 3 1

ISBN 0 00 220134 8

All photographs supplied by Natural Image. The copyright in the
photographs belongs to Bob Gibbons apart from the following:
M. Chinery 227; David Element 34, 35, 37, 38, 49, 79, 92, 94, 100,
115, 148, 247; Robin Fletcher 120; Alec S. Harmer 209; Roger Key
81; C. Nash 224; P. R. Perfect 55, 182; Peter Wilson 30, 31, 33, 40,
44, 47, 53, 68, 69, 73, 78, 85, 89, 107, 108, 110, 116, 117, 118, 130,
140, 143, 149, 155, 171, 173, 178, 181, 185, 193, 196, 207, 211, 212,
222, 223, 229, 238, 241

Title page photograph: Hawthorn Shieldbug

Artwork by Christina Hart-Davies

Typeset and designed by D & N Publishing
Lambourn Woodlands, Berkshire

Colour origination by Colourscan, Singapore
Printed and bound by Rotolito Lombarda SpA,
Milan, Italy

INTRODUCTION

Insects are all around us, in almost any environment we live in. They vary enormously in size from aphids, thrips and even smaller creatures which we can barely see, up to the largest butterflies, dragonflies and other insects which one cannot fail to notice. In general, there is a tendency to think of insects as all being rather unpleasant and harmful, neither attractive or useful. The reality could hardly be further from the truth, and the insect world is full of beautiful or beneficial insects, as well as many others that play their part in the complex processes that go on in the natural world. For example, bats rely almost exclusively on insects for their food, and most birds feed their young on insects and other invertebrates, as well as relying on them for food during much of the rest of the year. Without honey bees, bumble bees and other insects, little pollination would take place, and many crop yields would be vastly reduced or absent altogether. And for many people, the pleasure to be gained from seeing butterflies, dragonflies, and other insects, is enormous.

There are far more insects in Britain and northern Europe than could possibly be covered in a little book like this. In Britain alone, there are at least 20,000 species, many of them inconspicuous or very hard to identify without microscopic examination. In Europe as a whole, there are almost 100,000 species, with more waiting to be discovered or described. Therefore, this book is designed simply as an introduction to this fascinating world, picking out 240 species of insects and some insect relatives, with reference to almost as many again that are similar. They are a selection of the most conspicuous and readily identifiable members of our wealth of insect life. We have excluded butterflies and moths from this book, as they are covered in another guide in the series (see p.10), and in many other books, thus leaving more space for some of the less familiar insects. Conversely, we have included a small selection of invertebrates other than insects, such as spiders and harvestman, as these are not generally to be found in popular guides.

HOW TO USE THIS BOOK

The book describes and illustrates 240 of our commonest and most distinctive insects and other invertebrates, and refers to almost as many again. For each of the main entries, there is a clear colour **photograph** showing many of the distinctive features of the adult insect. Where males and females differ, the more identifiable one has been selected, usually the male. In a few cases, it is not the adult insect that is the most conspicuous feature of the life-cycle, and in these instances it is the more conspicuous phase that has been illustrated. For example, many galls such as the Robin's Pincushion gall (*see* p.179) are large and highly visible outgrowths on plants that are caused by tiny inconspicuous insects. Additional **artwork** has been used either to show other phases of the insect's life-cycle, or to illustrate key identification features in greater detail than shown in the photograph. In some instances, artwork is used to illustrate different but closely related species.

The accompanying **text** gives background information about the insect, including information about where it may be found, and general hints about how to identify it without detailed examination. The **ID Fact File** gives more detailed concise information about the key features of the insect, including its normal season when it may be seen. The dates given in the calendar bar are an indication only, and will vary according to location and season; finding an insect that fits the description but appears to be in the wrong season need not rule it out completely. For example, in the curious spring of 1998, dragonflies were appearing 2 months before their normal earliest date in some places.

The easiest way to use the book is to scan through the pictures looking for something that roughly matches the insect you have seen. If the picture and all the information fit, then the identification will almost certainly be correct; if some details do not quite fit, check the text for sexual differences, and the ID Fact File for common lookalikes. It is also worth checking adjacent pages, as related species are grouped together. There will, of course, be many instances where the insect cannot be precisely identified, though this book should give a rough idea of what family or group it belongs to.

The different orders, or groups, of insects are identified by a **symbol** at the top of the page, as an aid to quickly narrowing down the possibilities for any given insect. This follows the system used in the Collins Gem Insects Photoguide. The symbols, and orders which they refer to, are as follows:

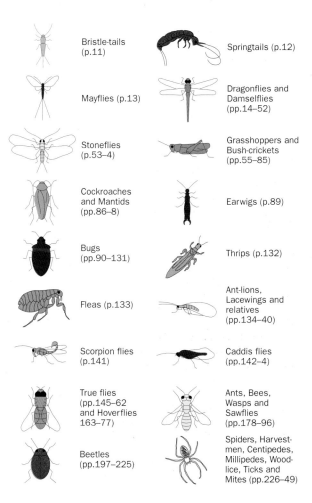

Bristle-tails (p.11)

Springtails (p.12)

Mayflies (p.13)

Dragonflies and Damselflies (pp.14–52)

Stoneflies (p.53–4)

Grasshoppers and Bush-crickets (pp.55–85)

Cockroaches and Mantids (pp.86–8)

Earwigs (p.89)

Bugs (pp.90–131)

Thrips (p.132)

Fleas (p.133)

Ant-lions, Lacewings and relatives (pp.134–40)

Scorpion flies (p.141)

Caddis flies (pp.142–4)

True flies (pp.145–62 and Hoverflies 163–77)

Ants, Bees, Wasps and Sawflies (pp.178–96)

Beetles (pp.197–225)

Spiders, Harvestmen, Centipedes, Millipedes, Woodlice, Ticks and Mites (pp.226–49)

FINDING INSECTS

Insects are to be found almost everywhere on land, even in winter, so it may seem odd, at first sight, to have a section on finding insects. However, much of the pleasure to be gained from looking at insects comes from finding particular groups of species, such as dragonflies, and being able to look at them closely, rather than simply seeing an unidentified tiny dark insect buzzing past you, so it makes sense to know how and where to find specific insects.

Without doubt, the best way to start finding insects is by finding good insect habitats. As a general rule, most insects like flowery, sheltered, undisturbed sites, with a good variety of vegetation such as a range of different trees and shrubs. In addition, many species need water – particularly clean, clear, well-vegetated, still water – at some stage in their life cycle. If you add the presence of old trees and fallen logs and branches – for many insects pass their larval stages in dead and dying wood – you have the recipe for a perfect site. Few places have all these qualities, of course, but there are particular types of sites that are worth looking out for, which have most of the qualities. Old woodland is especially good, particularly if there are flowery rides or clearings (or adjacent flowery fields), and a stream or pond. Heathland has a rather different range of species, many of which only occur on heaths. The best heaths have sandy soil with banks, where different bees and wasps can nest, and some damp or boggy areas. Another excellent habitat for insects is chalk grassland, especially on south-facing slopes, and where there is a certain amount of shelter from bushes or hedges. In mountain areas, the rough flowery grassland that occurs at 1000–2000 m altitude is exceptionally rich in insects. Finally, if you are interested in dragonflies or other insects that have a particular association with water, look for warm sheltered pools and lakes, with some aquatic vegetation. During the height of the summer, an early morning visit to such sites will almost certainly reveal emerging dragonflies, which can be watched at close quarters as they undergo the extraordinary transformation from aquatic nymph to adult insect.

It is always worth visiting nature reserves, whatever their habitats. Although very few are managed specifically for insects, they will almost certainly include a good range of more or less natural habitats, managed without the aid of damaging pesticides, and will have a good range of interesting insects.

Whatever habitat you are visiting, you will almost certainly see more insects by walking slowly and looking carefully at flower heads, or under leaves, and checking ahead for basking dragonflies or other insects. Insects are much less disturbed by slow, careful movements, and you can often approach very close to them in this way. It is well worth carrying some close-focusing binoculars, or a little monocular, to get a better view of the insects without approaching too closely. Insects are not usually associated with calls or other sounds, but if you start to listen hard, you realise that there are actually many insect sounds – grasshoppers, crickets, bush-crickets, cicadas, and even some beetles. All have clear songs, which differ from species to species. Also, the flight sounds of different groups are different, and with practice you can hear dragonflies, bumble bees – and mosquitoes and horse flies – before you see them!

By simply visiting a good site and looking and listening carefully, you will see a good range of insects. However, there are insects that will not show themselves readily by this approach, and they may need a more active method. For example, many insects are only active at night, and are very hard to find during the day. One good way to see moths, and some other night-flying insects, is by running a moth trap, which consists basically of a light set in a structure that allows attracted insects to fall into a box from which they cannot easily find their way out. For maximum attraction, a mercury vapour lamp is used. Such traps can be bought, made, or used at many field studies centres which operate entomological and natural history courses.

WHAT IS AN INSECT?

Insects are part of a huge tribe of invertebrate creatures known as the arthropods, which also includes the spiders, harvestmen, millipedes, crustaceans and many other groups, whose main characteristics include the possession of a hard external shell or skeleton, with flexible joints that allow the animal to move. Insects may be distinguished from all other arthropods (or 'invertebrates' as they are generally known) in several ways:

1. Most insects have wings at some time in their life cycle. Any invertebrate that has wings must be an insect, but there are a number of insects that do not have wings.

2. Insects normally have 6 legs in 3 pairs. Some insects have fewer legs (though never more), but they usually have 6 legs visible at some point in their life-cycle, or an indication of where the missing legs should be.

3. Insect bodies are divided into the head, thorax and abdomen. The head bears a pair of antennae, or feelers, though these may occasionally be very small, while the thorax bears the legs and wings. The abdomen is usually simple, though it may have structures associated with the mating process. When wings are present, they occur as one or two pairs. The true flies (Diptera – see pp.145) have only one pair of wings, with the second pair reduced to a pair of club-shaped structures known as halteres. This can be a useful way of separating bee- and wasp-mimicking flies, such as drone flies, from the real things, which always have 2 pairs of wings.

A few other groups of invertebrates are covered in this guide. Spiders (see p.226) are readily identifiable by having bodies that are divided into two distinct sections, and by the presence of 8 legs. Harvestmen (see p.241) are closely related, and also have 8 legs, but these are usually particularly long and thin, and the body is not divided into two sections. Other invertebrate groups are represented in the book simply by one or two typical species.

THE CONSERVATION OF INSECTS

The more we find out about insects in developed countries such as Britain, the more it becomes clear that many species have declined alarmingly over the past few decades. Any individual country will probably have a long list of insect species that have become extinct in recent years, and there are probably many more that became extinct before they were known about. Worse still, the decline in some species of birds and bats, amongst others, can be linked to the decline in their insect food. As we have found out more about the changes in insect populations, we have also discovered more about the requirements of insects, and these have often turned out to be alarmingly complex and demanding.

It is little wonder that insect conservation has lagged behind other branches of conservation. The vast numbers of species involved naturally means that detailed information is simply not available on where many of them are, how abundant they are, and exactly what conditions they require in order to survive. To complicate matters further, on any given site, it is almost inevitable that the species present will have conflicting requirements and it is almost impossible to cater for them all adequately. Until very recently, insect conservation has simply followed in the wake of other branches of conservation – that is, the conservation of suitable habitats for birds, mammals, flowers, amphibians and so on was expected to provide adequate habitats for most insects. More detailed knowledge in recent years has shown that specific habitats, or micro-habitats, need to be preserved specifically for insects, such as wet hollows in the forks of trees, damp muddy areas, dead and dying trees, and hollow stems of grasses and other plants during the winter. This means that nature reserves and other protected areas can be managed more with insects in mind. The first reserves established primarily for butterflies, and a few for dragonflies, are now well-accepted, though we are some way away from having specific hoverfly or ichneumon reserves! In the countryside as a whole, we need a reduction in the use of insecticides, and an increase in rough flowery areas and wetlands before insects can really make a come-back.

WHAT NEXT?

If you become interested in any or all of the branches of insects covered in this book, it is inevitable that, sooner or later, you will want more information. There are more detailed books available about insects as a whole, and about specific insect groups, such as dragonflies, ladybirds or hoverflies, and some are mentioned below. It is worth joining a society to go on outings with expert leaders, or receive useful information in newsletters. And finally, it is well worth going on courses that cover insects as their main or major feature. Some possible societies and field centres are listed below.

Societies
British Entomological and Natural History Society, c/o Institute of Biology, 20 Queensberry Place, London SW7 2DZ
British Dragonfly Society, The Haywain, Hollywater Rd, Bordon, Hampshire GU35 0AD
Butterfly Conservation, PO Box 222, Dedham, Essex CO7 6EY
The Wildlife Trusts, The Green, Witham Park, Waterside South, Lincoln LN5 7JR

Courses
Field Studies Council, Preston Montford, Montford Bridge, Shrewsbury SY4 1HW. Runs many courses around the country.
The Kingcombe Centre, Toller Porcorum, Dorchester DT2 0EQ. Offers a number of courses about, or including, insects.

Further Reading
Brooks, S. (ed). *Field Guide to the Dragonflies and Damselflies of Great Britain and Ireland*. British Wildlife Publishing, Hook, 1997
Chinery, .M. *Gem Insects Photoguide*. HarperCollinsPublishers, 1997
Chinery, M. *Pocket Guide Insects of Britain and Western Europe*. HarperCollinsPublishers, 1993
Gibbons, Bob. *Field Guide to the Insects of Britain and Northern Europe*. Crowood Press, Ramsbury, 1995
Still, J. *Wild Guide: Butterflies and Moths of Britain and Europe*. HarperCollinsPublishers, 1996

Silverfish

Lepisma saccharina

ID FACT FILE

SIZE:
Body length
12–18 mm

DESCRIPTION:
Smooth,
flattened but
cylindrical,
tapering
gradually from
head to tail.
Silvery-grey in
colour

FOOD:
Any decaying
carbohydrates
including paper
and food

LOOKALIKES:
The firebrat
*Thermobia
domestica* is
browner and
slightly larger

Silver-fish, so-called because of their silvery
scaly appearance, are fast-moving light-shun-
ning insects, often disturbed under furniture or
amongst old books in the home. They feed on
starchy scraps of food, or decaying paper or
material, disappearing rapidly if discovered.
They have flattened, tapering bodies, with two
long antennae, and three long segmented
'tails'. If picked up, they are very slippery to
the touch, as they quickly shed their surface
scales in your hand. They are widespread
throughout Europe.

Rock-pool Springtail
Lipura maritima

| J | F | M | A | M | J |
| J | A | S | O | N | D |

ID FACT FILE

Size:
2–3 mm long

Description:
Grey, with a tiny segmented cylindrical body, and short legs and antennae

Food:
Live or decaying plant material

Lookalikes:
Podura aquatica occurs in well-vegetated fresh water (*see* below)

The springtails are tiny wingless inconspicuous insects, and most have a special jumping organ, like a spring, which they can use to jump surprising distances if required. This species is more conspicuous than most, because it occurs in large groups on the surface of rock-pools and can be readily seen with the naked eye. It is one of the few springtails that does not possess a jumping spring, since this is not necessary in an aquatic environment.

mass of Rock-pool Springtails

Podura aquatica ×9

Green Drake or Common Mayfly

Ephemera danica

J	F	M	A	M	J
J	A	S	O	N	D

ID FACT FILE

SIZE:
About 50 mm
long, including
the tails

DESCRIPTION:
The body is
cylindrical,
yellowish-grey,
with darker
markings
towards the tip;
the wings are
clear with a band
of dark across
the centre of the
forewings

FOOD:
Organic debris,
in nymphal
stages only

LOOKALIKES:
There are several
similar species

Mayflies are a distinctive group, though
individual species are hard to identify. They
have two pairs of wings, with the front pair
much larger, and two or three very long 'tails'
at the end of the abdomen. They are unusual
amongst insects in having two phases that can
fly – the sub-adult, duller 'dun', which
transforms into the fully adult, brighter
'spinner'. The common mayfly is a large robust
species, with dark markings on the wings, and
three long tails.

J	F	M	A	M	J
J	A	S	O	N	D

White-legged Damselfly
Platycnemis pennipes

ID FACT FILE

SIZE:
Abdomen length
27–31 mm

DESCRIPTION:
Pale blue, with
black markings
on the abdomen,
and enlarged
white hind legs

FOOD:
Small insects
caught in flight

LOOKALIKES:
P. latipes (only in
SW Europe) is
even paler,
almost white

A medium-large damselfly, of which the males
have pale blue bodies marked with black, especially towards the tip of the abdomen, and distinctive white swollen sections (the tibiae) on
the hind legs, readily visible to the eye if close.
The females are similar but pale green to
white, without the black-tipped abdomen.
They prefer slow-flowing waters, though they
can turn up around almost any water body. It is
a common and widespread species through
much of Europe, though in Britain it is confined to the south.

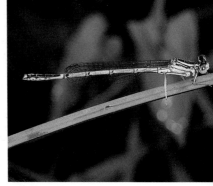

male White-legged Damselfly

close-up of the male's
enlarged hind legs, life-
size

J	F	M	A	M	J
J	A	S	O	N	D

ID FACT FILE

SIZE:
Abdomen length
25–29 mm

DESCRIPTION:
A predominantly
red species, but
with black legs,
black stripes on
the thorax, and
some black
towards the tip
of the abdomen.
Females similar,
but less slender,
and rather darker

FOOD:
Small insects
caught on the
wing

LOOKALIKES:
Small Red
Damselfly (p.16)

Large Red Damselfly
Pyrrhosoma nymphula

A medium-sized dragonfly that is one of the
earliest species to appear in the year, and one
of only two red and black species, so it can be
readily identified. It is rather a slow-moving
species, settling frequently, and easy to
approach. They occur, often abundantly,
around almost any water body except fast-
flowing rivers, and may be found throughout
Europe except the far north. In mountain
areas, they reach an altitude of about 1500 m.

DRAGONFLIES AND DAMSELFLIES, ODONATA

Small Red Damselfly

Ceriagrion tenellum

ID FACT FILE

SIZE:
Abdomen length
23–28 mm

DESCRIPTION:
A delicate red
species, with red
legs in both
sexes. Males are
almost all red
except for the
thorax, but
females have
extensive black
markings
towards the tip
of the thorax

FOOD:
Small insects,
caught on the
wing

LOOKALIKES:
Large Red
Damselfly (p.15)
which has black
legs

A slender, delicate and rather inconspicuous red damselfly, that rarely flies far and settles frequently. They are easy to approach, especially in cool weather, and they fly slowly away when disturbed. They are a mainly southern species, occurring from Germany southwards and only in the southern part of Britain; although they are rather local, they can be abundant where they do occur. The most favoured localities are shallow bog pools, though they do occur in other still waters.

male

J	F	M	A	M	J
J	A	S	O	N	D

Blue-tailed Damselfly

Ischnura elegans

ID FACT FILE

SIZE:
Abdomen length
22–29 mm

DESCRIPTION:
A predominantly
black or dark
blue species,
with blue stripes
on the thorax,
and a blue
segment at the
tip of the
abdomen.
Females are
rather variable in
colour and
pattern

FOOD:
Small insects

LOOKALIKES:
Scarce Blue-
tailed Damselfly
(p.18)

A distinctive medium-sized damselfly, easily
picked out by its combination of almost black
body except for a single segment of bright blue
near the tip. It is a common and widespread
species, occurring around most types of water
bodies, and able to withstand some degree of
pollution and salinity. They rarely stray far
from the marginal vegetation of their home
water body, and may be quite inactive in dull
weather. It occurs almost throughout Europe,
except for the far north and Spain.

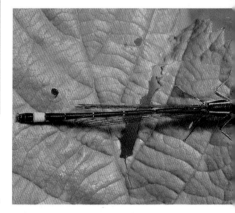

male

abdomens of Blue-tailed
Damselfly (above) and Scarce
Blue-tailed Damselfly ×4

Scarce Blue-tailed Damselfly

Ischnura pumilio

| J | F | M | A | M | J |
| J | A | S | O | N | D |

ID FACT FILE

Size:
Abdomen length
22–25 mm

Description:
Similar to Blue-tailed Damselfly
(p.17), but
smaller and
more slender,
and with the blue
of the 'tail'
extending across
two segments
(*see* diagram
p.17)

Food:
Small insects
caught on the
wing

Lookalikes:
Common Blue-tailed Damselfly
(p.17)

A delicate and rather slender damselfly, with a weak flight, rarely moving far and frequently settling low down in the vegetation. It differs from the much commoner common blue-tailed damselfly as described in the fact file. It occurs over much of Europe, though absent from most of Scandinavia and parts of western France and Spain. In Britain, it is a rare species, mainly found in the south. It occurs in a variety of habitats, including bog pools, water meadows, brackish coastal waters, and new gravel pits.

male

| J | F | M | A | M | J |
| J | A | S | O | N | D |

Red-eyed Damselfly

Erythromma najas

ID FACT FILE

SIZE:
Abdomen length
25–30 mm

DESCRIPTION:
The body is
mainly black, but
with a blue tip to
the abdomen,
and blue on the
sides of the
thorax. The eyes
are red in both
sexes. Females
are paler, without
the blue tip

FOOD:
Small insects
caught on the
wing

LOOKALIKES:
The Blue-tailed
Damselflies
(pp.17–18) look
rather similar,
but the red eyes
are quite
different

A robust and strong-flying damselfly, with a
distinctive combination of characteristics. As
its name suggests, it has red eyes unlike any
other damselflies except for one rather rare
relative. It is widespread through much of
Europe except the far south-west, and
northern Scandinavia; it is most likely to be
found in still well-vegetated water, with
abundant water-lilies or other floating leaves to
perch on. The females lay their eggs
underwater, whilst often still attached to a
male, and may submerge for long periods.

male

Common Blue Damselfly

Enallagma cyathigera

ID FACT FILE

SIZE:
Abdomen length 24–28 mm

DESCRIPTION:
Males are mainly blue, with black bands down the abdomen. Key features are the little 'ball on a stalk' on segment 2 of the abdomen, and the single black stripe on the side of the thorax (*see* below)

FOOD:
Small insects

LOOKALIKES:
Several damselflies of the genus *Coenagrion* (pp.21–22)

A medium-sized damselfly with a general appearance of being blue and black, like several other species. It is a robust damselfly, with relatively strong flight and marked aggressive tendencies towards similar species. It occurs abundantly in all sorts of water bodies, including brackish pools and flowing water, virtually throughout Europe except for the far south. It is also to be found at considerable altitudes in mountain and moorland areas, where it is sometimes the only species.

male

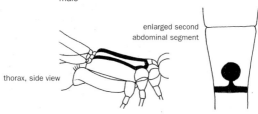

enlarged second
abdominal segment

thorax, side view

Azure Damselfly

Coenagrion puella

J	F	M	A	M	J
J	A	S	O	N	D

ID FACT FILE

SIZE:
Abdomen length
23–30 mm

DESCRIPTION:
Males are
banded blue and
black. All
Coenagrions
have an extra
black stripe on
the thorax which
is lacking in
Enallagma
(p.20), and this
species has a
black 'U' mark
on segment 2 of
the abdomen.
Females have
more black on
the abdomen

FOOD:
Small insects

LOOKALIKES:
Common Blue
Damselfly (p.20)
and other
Coenagrions
(p.22)

A medium-sized damselfly, predominantly blue and black in colour, without immediate distinguishing features. It occurs in a wide variety of aquatic habitats, especially ponds, sheltered lakes, canals, ditches and slow-flowing rivers, and is not normally associated with fast-flowing waters. Individuals may be encountered well away from water if there is suitable habitats such as wet meadows. It is widespread through all of Europe as far north as southern Scandinavia, and is common throughout.

male

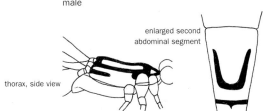

enlarged second
abdominal segment

thorax, side view

J	F	M	A	M	J
J	A	S	O	N	D

Variable Damselfly
Coenagrion pulchellum

A medium-sized damselfly, rather similar to the previous two species, and notoriously variable in markings (hence the name!). It is widespread in Europe from southern France northwards to the southern or coastal parts of Scandinavia, though it is rarely as common as the previous species. It occurs in similar habitats to the azure damselfly, though it can tolerate a wider range of water acidity. In favoured habitats, such as rough marshy areas with ditches and a slow river, it may be very abundant.

ID FACT FILE

SIZE:
Abdomen length
25–30 mm

DESCRIPTION:
Males are blue
and black, like
several other
species. Useful
distinguishing
marks include
the thin
interrupted blue
thorax stripes
(*see* below), and
the 'mercury'
mark on
abdomen
segment 2 (*see*
below). Females
tend to be
greener, with
uninterrupted
thorax stripes

FOOD:
Small insects
caught in flight

LOOKALIKES:
The previous two
species are very
similar, though
distinguishable
on close
examination

male

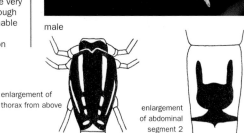

enlargement of
thorax from above

enlargement
of abdominal
segment 2

J	F	M	A	M	J
J	A	S	O	N	D

Emerald Damselfly

Lestes sponsa

ID FACT FILE

SIZE:
Abdomen length
26–32 mm

DESCRIPTION:
Overall, a bronze-
green insect, but
with powdery
blue patches on
the head, thorax
and tip of
abdomen in the
male (absent
from the female)

FOOD:
Small insects
caught on the
wing

LOOKALIKES:
The Scarce
Emerald *L. dryas*
is very similar,
slightly larger
and with just one
blue segment at
the abdomen tip
(not 1½ as in *L.
sponsa*). Very
rare in Britain but
widespread in
Europe

A medium-large damselfly, rather passive and
slow-moving in flight, rarely straying far from
its emergence site. They occur almost
throughout Europe, from north Spain and
north Italy to Finland, and are often abundant.
They can be found in a very wide range of
aquatic environments, but most commonly in
still, well-vegetated water bodies. All the *Lestes*
species (of which there are two in Britain and
six in Europe) settle with their wings half open,
at about 45° to the body, so they can be readily
distinguished from other damselflies.

male

J	F	M	A	M	J
J	A	S	O	N	D

Banded Demoiselle
Calopteryx splendens

ID FACT FILE

SIZE:
Abdomen length
34–40 mm

DESCRIPTION:
Males have
metallic blue
bodies, and
there is a large
smoky-blue patch
on each of the
four wings,
readily visible in
flight. Females
are green-bronze
and usually lack
the wing colour

FOOD:
Small insects
caught in flight

LOOKALIKES:
The
Mediterranean
Calopteryx *C.
haemorrhoidalis*
has similar
markings but a
red body; occurs
only in S Europe.
The following
species is also
similar

A large and very beautiful damselfly that can
occasionally be confused with a butterfly,
thanks to its coloured wings and buoyant flight.
They occur throughout central Europe from
north Spain and Italy northwards to central
Scandinavia. They are almost always associated
with flowing water, usually neutral to alkaline,
and may be particularly abundant along slow-
flowing, well-vegetated lowland rivers with fen
or damp meadows on either side. Males can be
quite aggressive, defending territory against
other males and some other insects.

male

J	F	M	A	M	J
J	A	S	O	N	D

Demoiselle Agrion
Calopteryx virgo

ID FACT FILE

SIZE:
Abdomen length
33–38 mm

DESCRIPTION:
Males are bluish-
green, with wings
that are wholly
blue-green in
colour. Females
are more brown
than those of the
banded, and the
wings are a
golden bronze

FOOD:
Small insects

LOOKALIKES:
Only the
preceding
species

This species is very similar to the banded
demoiselle in shape and habits (*see* Fact File for
differences). It is most frequent along faster
flowing smallish rivers, often acidic in character,
with abundant marginal vegetation, and shallow
gravelly patches. The females tend to be
sedentary, staying near the river they emerged
from, but males wander rather more widely, and
have similar territorial tendencies to banded
demoiselles. It is very widespread throughout
almost the whole of Europe, except for the drier
parts of Spain and northern Scandinavia.

male

J	F	M	A	M	J
J	A	S	O	N	D

Club-tailed Dragonfly
Gomphus vulgatissimus

ID FACT FILE

SIZE:
Abdomen length
33–37 mm

DESCRIPTION:
Both males and
females are
black and
yellowish-green.
This little group
of dragonflies
(the 'gomphids')
have widely
separated eyes,
whereas in other
dragonflies the
eyes touch. The
males have
distinctly club-
shaped abdo-
mens (hence
the name) but
females do not

FOOD:
Small insects

LOOKALIKES:
G. simillimus
(SW Europe only)
is more slender,
with less black

A medium-sized boldly marked dragonfly.
Compared with most dragonflies, both males
and females are rather sluggish, settling
frequently on vegetation or rocks, and rarely
flying far, though occasionally they will turn up
well away from water. It is almost always found
in association with large slow-moving rivers,
such as the Thames or Loire, where the larvae
live in the mud. It occurs patchily throughout
central Europe north of the Pyrenees as far
north as central Scandinavia. In Britain, it is
rare and mainly southern.

female

Slender Club-tailed Dragonfly

Gomphus pulchellus

J	F	M	A	M	J
J	A	S	O	N	D

ID FACT FILE

SIZE:
Abdomen length 34–38 mm

DESCRIPTION:
They have the widely spaced eyes of this group, but the body is particularly slender and only slightly club-tailed. Both sexes are similar, pale yellowish-green with dull black markings

FOOD:
Small to medium insects

LOOKALIKES:
G. simillimus has a more clubbed tail

A medium-sized but slender and rather weak-flying dragonfly. Both sexes fly slowly, rarely going far, and settling frequently, almost always on the ground. Their pale colour and restrained behaviour are reminiscent of an aged darter in autumn (*see* pp.46–50). Unlike other club-tailed dragonflies, they are almost always found around still water bodies, especially lakes and large ponds, where they may be quite abundant. They are most frequent in Spain, Portugal and south France, but can be found as far north as north Germany.

Onychogomphus forcipatus

ID FACT FILE

SIZE:
Abdomen length
32–38 mm

DESCRIPTION:
A boldly marked
yellow and black
insect. Males
have a strongly
clubbed tail, but
differ from the
club-tailed in
having conspic-
uous long brown
appendages at
the end of the
tail. Females are
similar in colour
but lack the
'club' and the
appendages

FOOD:
Small to medium
insects

LOOKALIKES:
O. uncatus (SW
Europe only) is
very similar,
distinguishable
by broader
stripes on the
thorax, and
bigger yellow
patches on the
abdomen

A medium-large dragonfly, with a distinctive appearance. They are almost always found close to rivers, including fast-flowing ones, where they spend most of their time sunbathing on stones or gravel banks. They can usually be approached quite closely and rarely fly far if disturbed. In particularly hot weather, they raise their abdomens towards the sun to try to keep cool. It is scattered throughout Europe, from Spain to Finland, though absent from large areas including Britain.

male

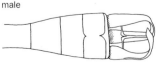

enlargement
male's apper
at the tip of t
abdomen

Golden-ringed Dragonfly
Cordulegaster boltonii

J	F	M	A	M	J
J	A	S	O	N	D

ID FACT FILE

SIZE:
Abdomen length 54–65 mm (females are longer than males)

DESCRIPTION:
Predominantly black, with narrow yellow rings on the abdomen, yellow stripes on the thorax, and green eyes. The female has a dagger-like ovipositor

FOOD:
A variety of insects

LOOKALIKES:
C. bidentata (mountain regions of S. Europe) differs in minor details, and has a black triangle between the eyes (not yellow)

A large and conspicuous dragonfly, with one of the longest bodies of any European insect. They are almost always associated with fast-flowing, well-oxygenated rivers and streams, where they breed, though both sexes are powerful fliers and can be found far from water at times. Although widespread virtually throughout Europe, from south Spain to Finland, they are rarely found in any quantity. The female lays eggs by hovering vertically over shallow water and stabbing her abdomen directly down into the gravel below.

male

J	F	M	A	M	J
J	A	S	O	N	D

Hairy Hawker
Brachytron pratense

ID FACT FILE

SIZE:
Abdomen length
40–46 mm

DESCRIPTION:
Males are
brownish-black,
with yellow
stripes on the
thorax, and blue
spots along the
abdomen.
Females are
similar, but
without stripes
and with yellow
spots. Both
sexes are
noticeably hairy

FOOD:
Small to medium
insects

LOOKALIKES:
Common Hawker
is similar (p.33),
but larger, later
and not hairy

The hairy hawker is a medium-sized dragonfly,
with a swift flight. Males tend to patrol their
territory, flying up and down a ditch or lake
margin, while females are less active. They settle
frequently on vegetation to feed or rest, and will
not usually fly far when disturbed. Unlike other
hawkers, they do not wander far, though in
windy weather they can be found sheltering
some way from water. They occur through most
of Europe, from the Pyrenees northwards to
Finland, though they are rarely abundant. Their
short early flight period is characteristic.

male

| J | F | M | A | M | J |
| J | A | S | O | N | D |

Brown Hawker

Aeshna grandis

ID FACT FILE

SIZE:
Abdomen length
54–60 mm

DESCRIPTION:
Predominantly
brown, with
orange-brown
suffusion on the
wings. Males are
darker, thinner
with a waist
edged by bright
blue. Females
are broader and
lack the blue

FOOD:
Medium to large
insects, including
butterflies

LOOKALIKES:
None

The Brown Hawker is a robust and impressive dragonfly, with beautiful coloration. The males, in particular, are tireless fliers, endlessly patrolling and quartering their home area, rarely settling during the day; fortunately, they can be identified from a distance by their brown bodies and conspicuous brown-veined wings. In cooler weather, or towards evening, they will settle on vertical surfaces such as trees. Apart from isolated localities in the Pyrenees, they occur mainly from central France northwards to north Scandinavia, and in the southern half of Britain.

female

J	F	M	A	M	J
J	A	S	O	N	D

Southern Hawker
Aeshna cyanea

ID FACT FILE

SIZE:
Abdomen length
51–60 mm

DESCRIPTION:
Males are
brownish-black,
with broad green
stripes on the
thorax, then
paired green to
blue spots all
down the
abdomen; the
last two pairs of
spots are both
merged into one.
Females similar,
but paler and
greener

FOOD:
Medium to large
insects

LOOKALIKES:
Other hawkers
especially *A.
viridis* (from
north Germany
northwards)
which is more
strongly blue,
and all the
abdominal spots
are in pairs

A large and conspicuous dragonfly. Southern Hawkers are extremely mobile insects which can turn up almost anywhere, including in towns, where their inquisitiveness may cause a few surprises. They will fly on in dull weather or semi-darkness, occasionally coming to lights like moths! When they do settle, they prefer vegetation especially trees and bushes, and may rest for long periods. Breeding sites are normally still or slow-moving water bodies of various types. Southern Hawkers are very widespread, from south Europe almost to the Arctic Circle.

female

Common Hawker
Aeshna juncea

| J | F | M | A | M | J |
| J | A | S | O | N | D |

ID FACT FILE

SIZE:
Abdomen length
51–57 mm

DESCRIPTION:
Males are
blackish with
yellow thorax
stripes and
paired blue spots
along the ab-
domen; females
are brown with
yellow spots.
Both sexes have
a yellow front
edge to the wing

FOOD:
Medium to large
insects, caught
on the wing

LOOKALIKES:
Other hawkers,
but especially *A.
subarctica* (NE
Europe only)
which is darker,
with blue or
green thoracic
stripes

The Common Hawker dragonfly is a large and
attractive insect, with bold, colourful markings.
Males are strong fliers, aggressively defending an
area if necessary, though several males may occur
in one site. Like other large hawkers, they may be
found well away from water. They most often
breed in mildly acidic, well-vegetated still waters,
from tiny moorland pools to large lakes,
particularly in upland areas. It is primarily a north
European species, abundant in Scandinavia,
Germany and Britain, but increasingly confined
to mountain areas further south.

male

Scarce or Migrant Hawker

Aeshna mixta

J	F	M	A	M	J
J	A	S	O	N	D

ID FACT FILE

SIZE:
Abdomen length
44–50 mm

DESCRIPTION:
Brown overall,
with no thorax
stripes and
variable bluish
spots down the
abdomen. There
is a yellow
triangle on
segment 2 of
the abdomen.
Females are
similar but duller

FOOD:
Medium to large
insects, caught
on the wing

LOOKALIKES:
Most similar to
A. affinis (S.
Europe only)
which has
brighter blue
markings

The Scarce Hawker is one of the smaller and least conspicuous of the hawkers, though it may often be very abundant. Males are less territorial in this species, and if you see several hawkers flying close together, it is probably this one. As the name suggests, the adults are migratory, moving mainly northwards from south Europe each year, though their resident range has extended northwards in recent years. It is widespread in Europe from Denmark and central Britain southwards, breeding mainly in lakes and ponds.

male

enlargement of
abdomen showing
yellow triangle

| J | F | M | A | M | J |
| J | A | S | O | N | D |

Emperor Dragonfly
Anax imperator

ID FACT FILE

SIZE:
Abdomen length
50–60 mm, with
males being the
larger

DESCRIPTION:
Males are
predominantly
bright turquoise
blue, with a
black stripe
along the
abdomen, and
green on the
head and thorax.
Females are
greenish-yellow
with brown
markings

FOOD:
Medium to large
insects, including
butterflies

LOOKALIKES:
Lesser Emperor
(p.36) is similar

The Emperor Dragonfly is one of the largest
and most impressive insects in Europe. They
are difficult insects to approach, as they are
constantly on the wing, most often out over
water, and when they do settle, it is often up in
a tree. Females are rather less active. Their
main habitat is larger ponds and lakes, or slow-
moving water such as canals, and it will survive
in brackish or slightly polluted waters. It is very
widespread and quite common throughout
southern and central Europe, as far north as
central England and southernmost Scandinavia.

male

Lesser Emperor Dragonfly

Anax parthenope

ID FACT FILE

SIZE:
Abdomen length
50–59 mm

DESCRIPTION:
More slender
than the
Emperor. Both
sexes have blue
only on a small
but conspicuous
patch at the top
of the abdomen;
otherwise, males
are greenish,
females are
yellow-brown,
with black
markings

FOOD:
Medium to large
insects

LOOKALIKES:
The Emperor
Dragonfly (p.35)

The Lesser Emperor is similar in general shape and habits to the Emperor, though slightly smaller and less boldly marked. It frequents similar habitats, though where the two occur together, it is usually harassed by its larger relative and occupies the less favourable parts. It is primarily an insect of southern Europe, from Switzerland and central France southwards, though in recent years it has been appearing in more northern localities including Britain, Holland and Germany.

female

Downy Emerald
Cordulia aenea

ID FACT FILE

SIZE:
Abdomen length
34–38 mm

DESCRIPTION:
Both sexes are
bronze-green to
almost black,
with a noticeably
downy thorax.
Males have a
moderately well-
marked waist
and clubbed tail

FOOD:
Small to medium
insects

LOOKALIKES:
Other species of
emerald are
similar (pp.38–9)

The Downy Emerald is a small to medium-sized dragonfly, with dark rather inconspicuous colouring, and it is easily overlooked. They tend to fly regularly up and down the same 'beat', along the margin of a lake or pond, often stopping to hover briefly; this means that if you see one passing, you can usually wait a few minutes and get a good close view as it returns. They are most frequent in still acid to neutral waters, commonly in woodland clearings, northwards from the Pyrenees and Alps as far as Finland.

J	F	M	A	M	J
J	A	S	O	N	D

Brilliant Emerald
Somatochlora metallica

ID FACT FILE

SIZE:
Abdomen length
37–40 mm

DESCRIPTION:
The overall
colour of both
males and
females is bright
metallic green,
with a downy
thorax, and
yellow spots on
the face

FOOD:
Small to medium
insects, caught
on the wing

LOOKALIKES:
The Northern
Emerald *S.
arctica* (which
occurs in
mountain areas
and the Arctic) is
darker, and the
males have
curved, not
straight,
appendages

The Brilliant Emerald is similar in form and
habits to the Downy Emerald (p.37), but – as
the name suggests – is a much brighter and
more metallic green colour. It occurs in
sheltered still or slow-flowing waters, especially
where there is some overhanging vegetation,
under which the female lays her eggs. It is
widespread in central and northern Europe
from the Pyrenees and Alps to the Arctic,
though it is rarely abundant where it does
occur. A slightly different form of the species
occurs in Greece and the Balkans.

appendages of male
Brilliant Emerald (left)
and Northern Emerald

| J | F | M | A | M | J |
| J | A | S | O | N | D |

Orange-spotted Emerald
Oxygastra curtisii

ID FACT FILE

SIZE:
Abdomen length
36–39 mm

DESCRIPTION:
Similar in form to
other emeralds,
dark green in
colour, but with a
band of
prominent
orange spots
along the
abdomen

FOOD:
Small to medium
insects

LOOKALIKES:
A distinctive
species

The Orange-spotted Emerald is a beautiful dragonfly, similar in form to the other emeralds, but with much more yellow or orange on the body. It differs from most emeralds in that it prefers slow-flowing water for breeding, such as canals and meandering rivers, often with some trees overhanging, though occasionally it occurs in lakes. It is highly sensitive to pollution. The Orange-spotted Emerald is a south-western species, occurring almost throughout France and Spain, but very rare elsewhere and extinct in Britain.

J	F	M	A	M	J
J	A	S	O	N	D

Four-spotted Chaser

Libellula quadrimaculata

ID FACT FILE

SIZE:
Abdomen length
27–32 mm

DESCRIPTION:
A distinctive
species,
yellowish-brown
overall with a
bold black tip to
the abdomen;
the wings have
yellowish veins,
and four black
spots in addition
to the basal
black triangle
that other
chasers have.
Males and
females are very
similar

FOOD:
Small or medium
insects, caught
on the wing

LOOKALIKES:
A distinctive
species

A medium-sized dragonfly, with a fast darting
flight. The males are very active, aggressively
defending their territory against other males
throughout the day, but regularly returning to
a perch by the water. They prefer still water,
usually acid to neutral, such as lakes, ponds
and bog pools, where they may become
extremely abundant in favourable conditions.
In certain years, large quantities may
migrate westwards from eastern Europe.
It occurs throughout Europe except in
the extreme south.

J	F	M	A	M	J
J	A	S	O	N	D

Scarce Chaser

Libellula fulva

ID FACT FILE

SIZE:
Abdomen length
26–29 mm

DESCRIPTION:
Males have a
powdery blue
abdomen (which
becomes marked
with black after
mating), and a
furry brownish
thorax. Females
are brown with
black markings.
The dark triangle
at the base of
each wing helps
distinguish them
from similar
skimmers
(pp.43–5)

FOOD:
Small insects

LOOKALIKES:
The Black-tailed
Skimmer (p.43),
and Broad-bodied
Chaser (p.42)
are both similar

The Scarce Chaser is a small and rather slender dragonfly, though with the active habits typical of this group. They settle regularly, particularly on stones and tree trunks, but dart off frequently at any sign of movement nearby. Females are more passive, and spend much time quietly resting or feeding away from water. Although scarce in Britain (hence the name), confined to the south and east, they are common through much of Europe from the Pyrenees north to Sweden, usually in slow-moving rivers and canals.

male

Broad-bodied Chaser
Libellula depressa

ID FACT FILE

SIZE:
Abdomen length
24–28 mm

DESCRIPTION:
Males are squat,
broad-bodied and
bright blue, with
only the very tip
of the abdomen
being coloured
black. Females
are yellowish-
brown. Both
sexes have well-
marked brown
triangles at the
base of the
wings

FOOD:
Small or medium
insects, caught
on the wing

LOOKALIKES:
The Scarce
Chaser (p.41)
and the Keeled
Skimmer (p.44)
are most similar

Although quite a small dragonfly, the Broad-
bodied Chaser can give the impression of a
larger insect thanks to its broad body and
strong flight. Males can be very aggressive,
often taking over a small pond and defending it
against all comers. Females are more passive,
spending much of their time away from water
except when mating. It is a common and
widespread species occurring virtually
throughout Europe except in the far north,
mainly preferring small to medium-sized still
water bodies with abundant vegetation.

female

J	F	M	A	M	J
J	A	S	O	N	D

Black-tailed Skimmer
Orthetrum cancellatum

ID FACT FILE

SIZE:
Abdomen length 30–35 mm

DESCRIPTION:
In males, the head and thorax are brown, while the abdomen is powdery blue tipped with black, but unlike the chasers, there are no dark triangles at the base of the wings in the skimmers. Females are dull yellowish-brown, marked with black

FOOD:
Small or medium insects

LOOKALIKES:
The Scarce Chaser (p.41) could be confused. Another skimmer, *O. albistylum* (central Europe only), has a very clear-cut black-tipped abdomen, as if dipped in ink, and notice-able white claspers

The Black-tailed Skimmer is a medium-sized dragonfly, with a strong rapid flight. Males settle frequently on the ground or other low surfaces, from where they make darting forays to feed or defend their territory. Females are more quiescent. Both sexes disperse widely, and find new water bodies, such as fish ponds, very quickly. It is common and widespread throughout most of Europe except for the far north, and the northern half of Britain. It is most frequent in still waters, including many artificial ponds and lakes.

male

Keeled Skimmer

Orthetrum coerulescens

ID FACT FILE

Size:
Abdomen length
27–30 mm

Description:
Males have dark
brown thorax
with two creamy
stripes, and a
powdery blue
abdomen with
just a hint of a
black tip.
Females are
orange-brown. As
with other
skimmers, there
are no dark
triangles at the
base of the
wings

Food:
Small to medium
insects

Lookalikes:
O. brunneum
(p.45) is most
similar

An attractive and rather graceful small
dragonfly, with less aggressive habits than its
close relatives. Males fly rather erratically along
the margins of water, often settling on the
ground or logs, flying up readily to investigate
any activity, though they are not noticeably
territorial. When settled, they hold their wings
forwards and downwards in a characteristic
way. It is most frequent in bog pools and other
still or slow-flowing waters. It is widespread
from south England and north France
southwards, but rare and local further north.

male

Orthetrum brunneum

ID FACT FILE

SIZE:
Abdomen length
29–31 mm

DESCRIPTION:
Similar in size
and shape to the
Keeled Skimmer
(p.44), but wholly
powdery blue,
including the
thorax. Females
are brownish,
very similar to
Keeled Skimmer

FOOD:
Small to medium
insects, caught
on the wing

LOOKALIKES:
Keeled
Skimmers (p.44)
are most similar

A smallish dragonfly, similar in general
appearance and habits to other skimmers. Males
are not particularly active, settling frequently on
the ground and making brief sorties to feed or
investigate activity. They can be approached
quite closely and will often return to the same
spot. It is essentially a warmth-loving south
European species, widespread in the southern
part of Europe, but becoming rarer northwards
and absent from Britain and Scandinavia. Its
normal habitat is still or slow-moving water,
with bare ground nearby.

male

J	F	M	A	M	J
J	A	S	O	N	D

Scarlet Darter
Crocothemis erythraea

ID FACT FILE

SIZE:
Abdomen length
22–29 mm

DESCRIPTION:
Males are
brighter red than
almost any other
European dragon-
fly, and the
bases of both
pairs of wings
are yellow-orange
in males and
females. Fe-
males are a dull
greyish-brown

FOOD:
Small to medium-
sized insects

LOOKALIKES:
Several darters
(pp.47–52) are
similar, but they
are generally
slightly more
slender, and less
bright

A smallish but rather robust dragonfly, conspicuous by virtue of its bright red colour in the males. They have similar habits to the darters (*Sympetrum* spp, *see* pp.47–51), settling regularly on or near the ground, and flying rather reluctantly, though they will defend territory at times. Their preferred habitat is still or slow-flowing water, including slightly saline sites. Their main range lies in southern Europe, though in certain years they migrate northwards, and have recently turned up in Britain.

male

J	F	M	A	M	J
J	A	S	O	N	D

Common Darter
Sympetrum striolatum

A small to medium dragonfly, which can be surprisingly inconspicuous. Males settle frequently on the ground or stones, rising frequently to attack other males or investigate possible prey. As the season progresses, they spend much of their time sunbathing, only rising lazily if disturbed. It is common and widespread throughout most of Europe except the far north, often very abundant in favoured localities. Its preferred habitats include lakes and ponds, which may be slightly brackish.

ID FACT FILE

SIZE:
Abdomen length
25–30 mm

DESCRIPTION:
Males are generally dull red in colour, with a brown abdomen. Females are dull yellowish brown. Both sexes have legs striped black and yellow longitudinally

FOOD:
Small or medium-sized insects

LOOKALIKES:
Other darters (pp.46 and 48–52). The Vagrant Darter *S. vulgatum* differs in tiny details, particularly longer black marks on its face. It is widespread from the Pyrenees northwards

mating pair

enlarged faces of
Common Darter (left)
and Vagrant Darter

J	F	M	A	M	J
J	A	S	O	N	D

Yellow-winged Darter
Sympetrum flaveolum

ID FACT FILE

SIZE:
Abdomen length
22–26 mm

DESCRIPTION:
Males are
orange-red in
colour, while
females are dull
yellowish brown.
Both sexes have
black and yellow
legs, but the key
feature is the
patches of yellow
at the base of
each wing

FOOD:
Small to medium
insects

LOOKALIKES:
The Red-veined
Darter (p.49) has
smaller yellow
patches, but the
red veins in the
wing are
distinctive

A distinctive dragonfly, similar in size and
general colour to many other darters, but
readily distinguishable by the broad area of
yellow colour suffusing the bases of all four
wings. It is a less aggressive species than the
Common Darter (p.47), flying more weakly,
and settling readily on vegetation or the
ground. Despite the weaker flight, it will
migrate over hundreds of miles at times, often
turning up in Britain and elsewhere in north
Europe. Its normal breeding habitat is in well-
vegetated slow-moving or still waters.

male

Red-veined Darter
Sympetrum fonscolombii

ID FACT FILE

SIZE:
Abdomen length
24–28 mm

DESCRIPTION:
Males are similar
to other darters,
but more pinkish-
red, and with the
distinctive red
veins on bluish
wings. Females
are duller
yellowish-brown,
but the wings are
still red-veined

FOOD:
Small to medium
insects, caught
on the wing

LOOKALIKES:
Most likely to be
confused with
the Yellow-
winged Darter
(p.48)

A smallish dragonfly, generally similar in
characteristics to other darters, but brighter
pink in colour and with red-veined wings.
Although males do perch readily on vegetation,
it tends to remain on the wing for longer than
most other darters, and feeds further out over
water. It also migrates over considerable
distances. Its main area of distribution, where
it is common, lies in south Europe, but it may
appear much further north, including in
Britain, at times. Its preferred breeding areas
are shallow, well-vegetated ponds and lakes.

male

J	F	M	A	M	J
J	A	S	O	N	D

Ruddy Darter
Sympetrum sanguineum

ID FACT FILE

SIZE:
Abdomen length
20–26 mm

DESCRIPTION:
Males are
brighter red than
most darters,
and with a
distinct 'waist'.
Females are the
normal yellowish-
brown. Both
sexes have black
legs, without the
yellow stripes

FOOD:
Small insects

LOOKALIKES:
*S. depressius-
culum* (central
Europe only) is
very similar,
differing in the
more finely
veined wings
and the more
flattened body

The Ruddy Darter is a typical darter, settling
frequently on the ground and making brief
sorties. It is less aggressive than the common
darter, and many males can occur close
together in a site. They are quite easily
approached, especially towards autumn, and
only fly a short distance. Their most usual
habitat is well-vegetated still or very slow-
flowing water, where they can become very
abundant. They are widespread through most
of Europe, and have slightly increased their
range in recent years.

male

Black Darter
Sympetrum danae

ID FACT FILE

SIZE:
Abdomen length
20–24 mm

DESCRIPTION:
Males are
essentially black,
though when
fresh they have
patches of yellow
on the thorax
and abdomen.
Females are
broader, and
brownish-black.
Both sexes have
black legs

FOOD:
Small insects

LOOKALIKES:
A distinctive
species

Although very similar in form and behaviour to
other darters, the Black Darter is quite
different in colour *(see* Fact File). Males are
not strongly territorial, and large numbers of
males, females and newly emerged specimens
can occur abundantly together in one site. Its
preferred habitat is bog and moorland with
pools, though it can occur in other still acid
waters with ample vegetation. It is a largely
northern species, widespread and abundant
from Britain and south Germany northwards,
but confined to mountains further south.

male

J	F	M	A	M	J
J	A	S	O	N	D

White-faced Darter

Leucorrhinia dubia

ID FACT FILE

SIZE:
Abdomen length
21–27 mm

DESCRIPTION:
Males are mainly
black, with bold
red markings on
the thorax and
along the
abdomen, while
females have
yellow markings
in place of red.
Both sexes have
a white face

FOOD:
Small insects

LOOKALIKES:
There are several
similar
Leucorrhinia
species in
eastern Europe,
with small
differences in
colour

A small and rather inconspicuous dragonfly,
with a weak flight, keeping low over vegetation.
Males hunt over water usually, displaying some
aggression to other males, but not strongly.
They frequently return to a marginal perch,
and will not usually fly far if disturbed. It is a
north-eastern species in Europe, common in
Scandinavia, Poland and Germany, but rare and
local elsewhere, and usually confined to boggy
areas on heaths and moors. It is not a very
mobile species, which means it is often absent
from seemingly suitable habitat.

male

J	F	M	A	M	J
J	A	S	O	N	D

Needle Fly

Leuctra fusca

ID FACT FILE

SIZE:
Body length
5–6 mm

DESCRIPTION:
Greyish brown
insects, with
translucent grey-
brown wings. The
antennae are
almost as long
as the body, but
the two tails
which are
conspicuous in
most stoneflies
are very short

FOOD:
Rarely feeds as
adult

LOOKALIKES:
There are several
similar species

The Needle Flies are so-called because their
wings are wrapped around their body when
they are at rest, forming a thin needle-like
tube. Like most stoneflies, they have long
antennae. They are essentially aquatic insects,
and the juvenile stages live in fast-flowing,
well-oxygenated, clean water, or occasionally in
lakes, throughout Europe. The adults are weak
fliers, and are unlikely to be found far from
their home river; they are most often seen
perched on tree trunks or stones near the
water, usually in shade.

J	F	M	A	M	J
J	A	S	O	N	D

Dinocras cephalotes

ID FACT FILE

SIZE:
Body length
15–20 mm
(male), up to
25 mm (female)

DESCRIPTION:
Both sexes are
greyish-black,
with long
antennae and
'tails' that
extend well
beyond the
folded wings

FOOD:
Feeds mainly in
the nymph stage,
on other
invertebrates

LOOKALIKES:
Perla bipunctata
is similar but
yellowish-grey.
Widespread.

This is one of the largest and most-often
noticed of the stoneflies, both as an adult and as
a nymph; even the empty nymph skin is quite
conspicuous. They occur in well-oxygenated
clean rivers, especially in upland and mountain
areas up to about 2000 m. The immature
nymph stages feed in the water, then emerge
onto a waterside stone to allow the adult to
break out, leaving the empty skin in place.
They are widespread through much of Europe,
though confined to mountains further south.

Large Marsh Grasshopper

Stethophyma grossum

J	F	M	A	M	J
J	A	S	O	N	D

ID FACT FILE

SIZE:
Body length up to 25 mm (male) and almost 40 mm (female)

DESCRIPTION:
They are basically greenish-brown, with red patches on the legs, and a yellow or cream stripe on each forewing

FOOD:
A variety of plant materials

LOOKALIKES:
The Large Banded Grasshopper *Arcyptera fusca* has more boldly marked legs, and occurs in mountain grasslands

This grasshopper is a large, bulky and relatively conspicuous insect. Both sexes can fly quite well and will often move 20–30 m if disturbed. Males emit a ticking noise as their call, audible from about 10m away. They occur in wet areas, especially bogs, fens and wet meadows, though not at high altitude. It is widespread through much of Europe northwards from the Pyrenees and Alps as far as the arctic; in Britain, it is uncommon and strongly southern in distribution.

J	F	M	A	M	J
J	A	S	O	N	D

Rufous Grasshopper
Gomphocerippus rufus

ID FACT FILE

SIZE:
Body length up to 16 mm (male), 24 mm (female)

DESCRIPTION:
Although generally brown in colour, it is readily recognisable by its clubbed, white-tipped antennae, particularly noticeable in males

FOOD:
Vegetation, especially grasses

LOOKALIKES:
No closely similar species

A medium-sized grasshopper. Rufous Grasshoppers occur mainly in forest clearings and margins, in damp or dry conditions, though they may also occur in open grassland at times. They leave the ground more readily than most grasshoppers, and often sun themselves on bushes. The song is a gentle clockwork purring, lasting for about five seconds. It is moderately common and widespread in Europe from the Alps and Pyrenees north to central Scandinavia; in Britain, it is rare and strongly southern.

J	F	M	A	M	J
J	A	S	O	N	D

Mottled Grasshopper

Myrmeleotettix maculatus

ID FACT FILE

SIZE:
Body length up to
12 mm (male),
17 mm (female)

DESCRIPTION:
Very variable, but
mottled with
some mixture of
brown, green,
black and white.
A distinctive
feature is the
male's antennae
which bend
outwards at the
tips, and are
slightly clubbed

FOOD:
Low vegetation

LOOKALIKES:
*Omocestus
haemorrhoidalis*
is similar, but
the males lack
the clubbed
antennae

The Mottled Grasshopper is one of the
smallest grasshoppers in Europe, but is quite
conspicuous by virtue of its bold colouring
and distinctive call. The song is reminiscent of
a watch being wound, in a series of
increasingly loud wheezes. Its preferred
habitat is in areas where there is bare soil,
especially on sandy heaths and dunes, more
rarely on dry grassland. It is widespread
throughout most of Europe except the
extremes, though always local, restricted by
lack of suitable habitat.

mating pair

Common Field Grasshopper

Chorthippus brunneus

ID FACT FILE

SIZE:
Body length up to 18 mm (male), 25 mm (female)

DESCRIPTION:
A variable but generally brownish insect, with wings stretching well beyond the abdomen tip. The upper side of the tip of the abdomen is usually reddish, especially in males

FOOD:
Low vegetation, mainly grasses

LOOKALIKES:
The Bow-winged Grasshopper *C. biguttulus* has a markedly curved front edge to the forewing, especially in males. Widespread in north Europe, but absent from Britain

A medium-sized grasshopper, with noticeably long wings, and it flies more readily than most grasshoppers. It occurs in warm dry areas with short turf, such as chalk or limestone grassland, and not infrequently on mown lawns. The call is a short harsh buzz, lasting less than half a second, and repeated at 2–3 second intervals, with other males replying if they are nearby. It occurs throughout much of the central part of Europe, from the Pyrenees to Finland, and it is widespread and common in Britain.

J	F	M	A	M	J
J	A	S	O	N	D

Meadow Grasshopper
Chorthippus parallelus

ID FACT FILE

SIZE:
Body length up to
16 mm (male),
23 mm (female)

DESCRIPTION:
Generally green
in colour, and
most distinctive
by virtue of the
fact that even
fully mature
adults, of both
sexes, have very
short wings,
though the
male's are
slightly longer

FOOD:
Grass and other
vegetation

LOOKALIKES:
C. montanus is
similar but the
wings are
distinctly longer
and the call is
slower. Wet
meadows in
Europe, not UK

This smallish insect is probably the commonest
and most familiar of grasshoppers. It can occur
in a wide variety of grassy habitats, with a
preference for damper, lusher grasslands
where the sward is longer. It can even survive,
at least for a while, in lush heavily fertilised
agricultural grasslands. It occurs very widely in
northern Europe, including most of Britain,
though further south it tends to only occur in
mountain areas. Its call, redolent of summer
days, is a burst of rough scraping sounds lasting
for about a second.

male (top) and female
Meadow Grasshoppers
showing the typical
upturned abdomen of a
male grasshopper

Lesser Marsh Grasshopper

Chorthippus albomarginatus

J	F	M	A	M	J
J	A	S	O	N	D

ID FACT FILE

SIZE:
Body length up to 15 mm (male), 20 mm (female)

DESCRIPTION:
Generally greenish to brownish with wings that do not quite reach the end of the abdomen. Females (*see* photo) have a prominent creamy-white stripe along the margin of the forewings

FOOD:
Grass and other vegetation

LOOKALIKES:
The Steppe Grasshopper *C. dorsatus* is similar, with slightly longer wings, no stripe, and (usually) a reddish tip to the abdomen. Widespread in Europe, not in UK

A small to medium grasshopper with few obvious distinguishing features at first glance. It occurs in coastal marshlands, including saltmarshes, and in other wet meadows. It is a common species throughout much of Europe from central Scandinavia southwards, though in Britain it is mainly coastal and southern. The call consists of three equally loud short chirps, though there is sometimes a different call when two males are close together. The Lesser Marsh Grasshopper is not a proficient flier, and rarely goes far if disturbed.

GRASSHOPPERS AND BUSH-CRICKETS, ORTHOPTERA

Common Green Grasshopper

Omocestus viridulus

J	F	M	A	M	J
J	A	S	O	N	D

ID FACT FILE

SIZE:
Body length up to
17 mm (male),
24 mm (female)

DESCRIPTION:
Variable in
colour, but usual-
ly mainly green.
Abdomen never
red-tipped. Males
usually have dark
sides to the
forewings

FOOD:
Grasses

LOOKALIKES:
None closely
similar

The Common Green Grasshopper is an
attractive and familiar species, occurring in
most types of grassland, particularly dry ones
such as chalk downland where it may be very
abundant. It occurs almost throughout Europe,
widespread in the north but increasingly
confined to mountains in the south. The call is
quite distinctive, a loud ticking sound which
increases in volume for about 8–10 seconds,
then 'plateaus out' for a roughly equal length
of time (unlike its close relative the Woodland
Grasshopper, p.62, which has the first part of
the call but not the second).

J	F	M	A	M	J
J	A	S	O	N	D

Woodland Grasshopper
Omocestus rufipes

ID FACT FILE

SIZE:
Body length up to
17 mm (male),
21 mm (female)

DESCRIPTION:
Males are
distinctive, with a
bright red tip to
the abdomen
then yellowish
towards the
middle. Parts of
the legs are red,
and the tips of
the palps (part of
the mouthparts)
are white. The
general colour is
dark brown.
Females are
much greener

FOOD:
Grass and other
plant material

LOOKALIKES:
None

An attractive and quite distinctive small to
medium-sized grasshopper. In Britain, its
preferred habitat tends to be woodland
margins and clearings (hence the common
name), but elsewhere it also occurs in dry open
grasslands or the open areas of heaths. The call
resembles that of the Common Green
Grasshopper (p.61), but is truncated, leaving
only the rising part. It is widespread in Europe
except for much of Scandinavia, and is rare in
the far south. In Britain it is uncommon and
strongly southern.

male

Club-legged Grasshopper
Gomphocerus sibiricus

J	F	M	A	M	J
J	A	S	O	N	D

ID FACT FILE

SIZE:
Body length up to
23 mm (male),
25 mm (female)

DESCRIPTION:
Variable in
colour, but
usually green or
brown. Males are
very distinctive
for two reasons –
they have greatly
swollen front
tibiae on their
legs, and club-
shaped but
flattened
antennae.
Females are best
identified by
association with
males

FOOD:
Grass and other
vegetation

LOOKALIKES:
None

A medium-sized very distinctive grasshopper.
It occurs almost exclusively in mountain
pastures, particularly where there is ample
bare ground on which they cluster for warmth.
It is most frequent at about 2000 m, but can
occur up to almost 3000 m despite the long
snowy winters. The Alps and the Pyrenees are
its main home, though it occurs in other
mountain areas, but not in Britain. Its call is
complex and variable, depending on the
circumstances, but usually lasts for about 20
seconds in a staccato burst.

mass of Club-legged Grasshoppers basking

male Club-legged
Grasshopper showing
enlarged front legs and
clubbed antennae

Stripe-winged Grasshopper
Stenobothrus lineatus

J	F	M	A	M	J
J	A	S	O	N	D

ID FACT FILE

SIZE:
Body length up to 20 mm (male), 26 mm (female)

DESCRIPTION:
Generally greenish, more rarely brown. Both sexes have a prominent white comma-like mark on the forewings, and females have a white stripe along the edge of the forewing

FOOD:
Vegetation, especially grass

LOOKALIKES:
The Lesser Mottled Grasshopper *S. stigmaticus* is smaller, with less marked commas. Very rare in Britain, more frequent in central Europe

A medium to large grasshopper. It occurs in a variety of dry habitats, especially chalk and limestone grassland, or dry grazed heathland, and less frequently in damper grassland. It is widespread through Europe from south Scandinavia southwards, but largely confined to mountains in the far south. In Britain, it is local and southern only. Its call is a distinctive wheezing that rises and falls in pitch, and lasts for about 15 seconds, though there is also a quieter courtship song when a female is close by.

wing of Stripe-winged Grasshopper showing prominent white 'comma'

J	F	M	A	M	J
J	A	S	O	N	D

Rattle Grasshopper

Psophus stridulus

ID FACT FILE

SIZE:
Body length up to 25 mm (male), 40 mm (female)

DESCRIPTION:
Generally brownish-grey to black (males are darker), but with hindwings that are almost entirely red, with a brown tip, but visible only when they fly

FOOD:
Grasses

LOOKALIKES:
The Red-winged Grasshopper (p.66) is very similar

A largish grasshopper that is one of a small group of species that exhibit 'flash coloration': they are dull in colour, but when they fly, they show bright red (or blue in some species) underwings, which disappear as they settle. The confused predator searches for a colourful insect and fails to find it. This species lives in warm dry grassy places, often with bare stony ground, in lowland and lower mountain areas. It is widespread from south Sweden to Spain and Italy, but absent from Britain. When the males fly, they produce a loud rattling sound.

wings as if in flight, showing the red hind wing

GRASSHOPPERS AND BUSH-CRICKETS, ORTHOPTERA

Red-winged Grasshopper

Oedipoda germanica

J	F	M	A	M	J
J	A	S	O	N	D

ID FACT FILE

SIZE:
Body length up to
21 mm (male),
28 mm (female)

DESCRIPTION:
Most frequently
dark brown
banded with
lighter brown.
The hindwings
are red, with a
broader marginal
brown band than
the Rattle
Grasshopper.
There is also a
difference in the
shape of the
pronotum in each
species (*see*
below)

FOOD:
Low-growing
vegetation

LOOKALIKES:
The Rattle
Grasshopper is
most similar

A medium-sized grasshopper that shares with the previous species the characteristic of having a well-camouflaged body at rest and bright red wings on display when it flies. It can only be distinguished by close examination (*see* Fact File), or familiarity. However, unlike the Rattle Grasshopper, this species does not produce a dry rattle when it flies. It occurs mainly in warm south-facing slopes, usually with bare ground, and often on limestone. It is a southern species, reaching north to central Germany.

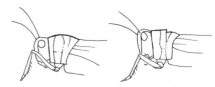

enlarged thorax area, showing curved pronotum
of Rattle Grasshopper (left) and indented
pronotum of Red-winged Grasshopper

Blue-winged Grasshopper

Oedipoda caerulescens

J	F	M	A	M	J
J	A	S	O	N	D

ID FACT FILE

SIZE:
Body length up to 21 mm (male), 28 mm (female)

DESCRIPTION:
The overall body colour is banded darker and lighter brown. The hindwings are blue, as described in the text

FOOD:
Low-growing grasses and herbs

LOOKALIKES:
Sphingonotus caerulans has paler blue wings without the dark borders. It has a similar distribution

A medium-sized grasshopper that is extremely similar in general characteristics to the preceding species, except that its wings are blue edged with brown and with a translucent tip. In fact, the females are so similar that males of one species may approach the female of the other, though they are not known to cross-breed. It occurs in a variety of warm dry places from southern Sweden throughout the rest of Europe (though absent from Britain), and is less demanding than the red species.

J	F	M	A	M	J
J	A	S	O	N	D

Locust
Locusta migratoria

ID FACT FILE

SIZE:
Body length
32–55 mm

DESCRIPTION:
In the solitary
phase, they are
mostly green and
grey, with
reddish sections
on the hind legs.
The wings extend
well beyond the
body, but in the
migratory phase
they are even
longer

FOOD:
Vegetation

LOOKALIKES:
The Egyptian
Grasshopper
(p.69) is very
similar in size,
but has striped
eyes

The Locust, or Migratory Locust, is one of the largest of European grasshoppers. Its life-cycle has a curious feature, in that it can occur in two forms; normally, it occurs as the sedentary solitary locust, which does not travel far. However, when population pressures become strong, they develop into a structurally different migratory phase, which is much more active and can give rise to the damaging locust swarms (now very rare in Europe). In Europe, it is a southern species, almost always found as the solitary phase, though occasionally it migrates to north Europe.

female Locust, solitary phase

| J | F | M | A | M | J |
| J | A | S | O | N | D |

Egyptian Grasshopper
Anacridium aegyptium

ID FACT FILE

SIZE:
Body length up to 40 mm (male) or 65 mm (female)

DESCRIPTION:
Predominantly mottled greyish-brown, distinctly bulky. Distinguishable from Locust by the vertically striped eyes, which are quite conspicuous, and other small details. The immature stages are green

FOOD:
Vegetation of various types

LOOKALIKES:
Locust (p.68)

The Egyptian Grasshopper is as large and impressive as the Locust, and more likely to be seen in Europe than the Locust, though only in the south. They can fly well, but normally only over short distances, and they never form swarms or cause significant damage. They are virtually silent, without obvious calls. It is a southern species, occurring almost throughout south Europe, including many of the islands, and it will occasionally turn up further north, perhaps brought in accidentally.

Common Ground-hopper

Tetrix undulata

ID FACT FILE

SIZE:
Body length
8–11 mm

DESCRIPTION:
Mottled brownish
in colour (though
occasionally
pinkish or
yellowish), with
an arched
pronotum that
reaches just
beyond the end
of the abdomen

FOOD:
Low vegetation

LOOKALIKES:
There are several
other ground-
hoppers, mostly
with longer
pronotums

The ground-hoppers are a small group, resembling small grasshoppers, but differing in having a pronotum (the shield behind the head) which extends at least to the end of the body and often beyond, though some species are still able to fly. The Common Ground-hopper occurs widely in damp grassy places such as meadows or woodland clearings, though it is easily overlooked. It is widespread in Europe from north Spain northwards, and throughout most of Britain, where it is easily the commonest ground-hopper.

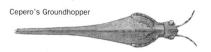

Cepero's Groundhopper

J	F	M	A	M	J
J	A	S	O	N	D

Speckled Bush-cricket

Leptophyes punctatissima

ID FACT FILE

SIZE:
Body length
10–17 mm, with
males being the
larger

DESCRIPTION:
Almost entirely
green in colour,
finely speckled
reddish-brown.
The antennae
are very long, as
with most bush-
crickets, and the
ovipositor is
sickle-shaped
and green (*see*
below)

FOOD:
Foliage

LOOKALIKES:
There are several
other similar
species in
Europe, but in
Britain only Oak
Bush-cricket
(p.72) is at all
similar

The Speckled Bush-cricket is a small and
rather inconspicuous green species which
blends easily into the vegetation where it lives.
Its preferred habitat is dense bushy
undergrowth such as brambles and nettles,
particularly along woodland margins, and it
also occurs in parks and gardens. Although
common, it is usually only found by chance,
especially if it wanders into a house. Its call is
so quiet as to be insignificant to humans. It
occurs throughout Europe, from central
Scandinavia southwards.

female

the short curved ovipositor
of Speckled Bush-cricket

J	F	M	A	M	J
J	A	S	O	N	D

Oak Bush-cricket
Meconema thalassinum

ID FACT FILE

SIZE:
Body length
12–15 mm

DESCRIPTION:
Mainly pale
green with a
short brown and
yellow mark at
the base of the
pronotum. The
females have a
long, slightly
curved oviposi-
tor, which is over
half the length of
the body

FOOD:
Arboreal
vegetation

LOOKALIKES:
The Southern
Oak Bush-cricket
M. meridionale
has shorter
wings and
ovipositor. It
occurs from
C France and
S Germany
southwards

A delicate green bush-cricket, with a much
more slender body than most similar species. It
spends most of its life in trees such as oak and
other deciduous trees, and is only active at
night, so it tends not to be noticed in its natural
habitat. However, they come frequently to
house lights from nearby trees. It is very
widespread in Europe from southern Sweden
almost to the extreme south; in Britain it is
common only in the south. Its call is made by
drumming on a leaf with its hind legs – not
surprisingly, this is barely audible to humans!.

female

Short-winged Conehead

Conocephalus dorsalis

| J | F | M | A | M | J |
| J | A | S | O | N | D |

ID FACT FILE

SIZE:
Body length
11–17 mm

DESCRIPTION:
Mid-green in
colour with a
brown stripe
along the back.
Normally the
wings only reach
about halfway
along the
abdomen, though
long-winged
forms occur. The
dagger-like
ovipositor is
distinctly curved

FOOD:
Plant material

LOOKALIKES:
Long-winged
Conehead (p.74)

A small slender bush-cricket, with antennae
that are about three times as long as the body.
It is most frequent in slightly damp rough
pastures where there is some long vegetation.
In Britain, it is largely coastal, and particularly
favours the upper parts of saltmarshes. It is
widespread through most of Europe, except
the extreme north and south. The call is
reminiscent of a quiet sewing machine, but
differs from the Long-winged Conehead (p.74)
in changing pitch to a deeper song every few
seconds then back again.

female

J	F	M	A	M	J
J	A	S	O	N	D

Long-winged Conehead
Conocephalus discolor

ID FACT FILE

SIZE:
Body length
12–17 mm

DESCRIPTION:
Very similar to
the Short-winged
– green with a
brown stripe –
but the wings are
much longer,
extending well
beyond the
abdomen tip,
and the
ovipositor is
longer and
almost straight

FOOD:
Vegetation

LOOKALIKES:
Short-winged
Conehead (p.73),
and the Large
Conehead
Ruspolia nitida
which has even
longer and more
robust wings,
and a body
length of up to
29 mm. From
Germany
southwards

This bush-cricket is very similar to the Short-winged Conehead (p.73) differing in a few morphological details (*see* Fact File) and its slightly different song. The call is just like a quiet sewing-machine, purring along in the undergrowth, without significant variation in pitch. Unfortunately, it is quite quiet, and many people cannot hear it. It is a widespread species of rough grassland and reed-beds, particularly near rivers and marshes. It is slightly more warmth-demanding than the short-winged, and occurs from north Germany southwards, including southern Britain.

female

ovipositors of Long-winged (left)
and Short-winged Coneheads

Great Green Bush-cricket

Tettigonia viridissima

ID FACT FILE

SIZE:
Body length up to
42 mm, with the
wings
considerably
longer

DESCRIPTION:
Green, except for
a brown stripe
down the back.
The long robust
wings extend
about half as far
again beyond the
abdomen tip. The
ovipositor is
about 2 cm long,
slightly down-
curved, reaching
almost to the
tips of the wings

FOOD:
Omnivorous,
mainly
invertebrates

LOOKALIKES:
The Upland
Green Bush-
cricket *T.
cantans* is
slightly smaller
with wings only
reaching just
beyond the
abdomen.
Upland pastures,
not Britain

This impressive insect is the largest bush-cricket in north Europe, and one of the largest in Europe. You can often sense it moving through vegetation by the bending branches, before you actually see it! Despite its bulk, it is surprisingly hard to see. The call is characteristic, like a freewheeling bicycle, audible from a considerable distance, and emitted from around midday to the middle of the night. It occurs in a variety of bushy habitats, though in Britain it is largely coastal. It can be found almost throughout Europe except the far north and at higher altitudes.

female

| J | F | M | A | M | J |
| J | A | S | O | N | D |

Wart-biter

Decticus verrucivorus

ID FACT FILE

SIZE:
Body length
24–44 mm, with
females larger
than males

DESCRIPTION:
A greenish, bulky
insect, mottled
with grey and
brown, though
variable. The
eyes are dark
brown (those of
the Great Green
(p.75) are
green). The
ovipositor is
long, brown,
slightly upcurved

FOOD:
Omnivorous

LOOKALIKES:
The Heath Bush-
cricket
*Gampsocleis
glabra* is smaller
and less robust
with pale brown
wings. Central
Europe, not
Britain

This is another large bush-cricket, almost as
large as the Great Green (p.75), though its
wings are shorter. It is more of a ground-
dwelling insect, occurring in low vegetation
with bare areas, such as heaths, chalk
grassland and mountain pastures. It is
widespread in Europe except for the far south,
but is extremely rare in Britain in just a few
southern localities. The call is a series of
ticking sounds which gradually speed up
though always remaining distinct, emitted
mainly in warm sunny weather.

female

J	F	M	A	M	J
J	A	S	O	N	D

ID FACT FILE

SIZE:
Body length
12–18 mm

DESCRIPTION:
A dark insect,
predominantly
dark brown with
green on the
head and top of
the pronotum,
though it can
vary. The wings
are short,
reaching about
halfway along the
abdomen

FOOD:
Omnivorous

LOOKALIKES:
Dark Bush-cricket
(p.79) can look
similar

Bog Bush-cricket
Metrioptera brachyptera

A short but quite bulky bush-cricket. The Bog-
Bush cricket occurs in a variety of damp, and
occasionally dry, vegetation types, and is by no
means confined to bogs (though in Britain, it is
most likely to be found on bogs or wet heaths).
It is widespread throughout Europe from
northern Scandinavia southwards, but absent
from the far south. In Britain, it is absent from
most of Scotland and generally rarer in the
north. The call is not particularly distinctive – a
series of short guttural chirps, only audible
from a few metres away.

male

J	F	M	A	M	J
J	A	S	O	N	D

Roesel's Bush-cricket

Metrioptera roeselii

ID FACT FILE

SIZE:
Body length
14–18 mm

DESCRIPTION:
Squat, slightly
hunched insect,
greenish brown
in colour. The
most distinctive
feature is the
white or pale
green margin to
the pronotum
flaps (*see*
photo). The
wings reach
about halfway
along the body;
the ovipositor is
short and
upcurved

FOOD:
Omnivorous,
mainly plant
material

LOOKALIKES:
The markings are
distinctive. Bog
Bush-cricket
(p.77) is similar
in shape

A smallish but bulky bush-cricket, very similar
in size and shape to the Bog Bush-cricket. Its
preferred habitat is tall grassland, dry to damp,
but very often in association with river valleys,
and it can be very abundant in suitable
localities. In Britain, it is mainly coastal and
southern, though it has spread inland in recent
years. It is widespread and abundant through
most of Europe except the far south and north.
The call is unusual, perhaps more like that of a
cicada than a bush-cricket – a uniform high-
pitched buzzing that continues for long periods.

male

Dark Bush-cricket
Pholidoptera griseoaptera

ID FACT FILE

SIZE:
Body length
13–18 mm

DESCRIPTION:
Predominantly
brown or greyish-
brown, but with a
striking yellow
underside. The
ovipositor is
brown, upcurved,
and about
10 mm long

FOOD:
Omnivorous

LOOKALIKES:
The Alpine Dark
Bush-cricket *P.
aptera* is slightly
larger, more
reddish, with a
creamy back
edge to the
pronotum. In
mountains of
central Europe

A small but squat species of bush-cricket. It is
very common and widespread, though its habit
of skulking in vegetation and being active at
night means that it is hardly ever seen. It occurs
almost throughout Europe except in the extreme
south, and is common in the southern part of
Britain. Its preferred habitat always includes
some rough dense herbage such as bramble
patches, and it can occur in woodland clearings,
parks, gardens and elsewhere. The call is a short
buzz (which slows into three separate syllables in
cooler weather), often heard at night.

female

Saddle-backed Bush-cricket or Zi-zi

Ephippiger ephippiger

J	F	M	A	M	J
J	A	S	O	N	D

ID FACT FILE

SIZE:
Body length
22–30 mm

DESCRIPTION:
Predominantly
green, with
yellowish wing
vestiges and a
patch of black
behind the head,
though the
ground colour
can vary. The
ovipositor is
narrow, curved
upwards, and
almost as long
as the body

FOOD:
Omnivorous, and
may occasionally
be a pest on
crops

LOOKALIKES:
There are several
similar species
in southern
Europe

This is one of a little sub-family of bush-crickets in which the pronotum is expanded and raised up, like a saddle (hence the name). In north Europe, this species is quite distinctive, though further south there are other related species. It occurs sparingly in the Low countries and south Germany, becoming more frequent southwards, in a variety of dry sunny habitats. Its call reflects the second common name, being a double buzz, 'zi-zi'. It is active during the day and night.

male

ovipositor of Zi-zi,
approximately life size

| J | F | M | A | M | J |
| J | A | S | O | N | D |

House Cricket
Acheta domestica

ID FACT FILE

SIZE:
Body length
16–20 mm

DESCRIPTION:
Brown or
yellowish-brown,
with sculptured
wing surfaces.
The wings project
beyond the end
of the body in
two spikes when
rolled and folded

FOOD:
Omnivorous,
including refuse
and stored food

LOOKALIKES:
There are several
rather similar
native species,
such as the
Wood-cricket
(p.83)

The House Cricket is a relatively well-known
insect, thanks to its habit of living in close
proximity to man, in houses and other warm
buildings, and on refuse tips. It is considered
to be a pest (though not normally harmful)
and is often subject to control measures. Its
call is a mellifluous, almost bird-like, warble,
produced mainly in the evening and at night.
It is widespread in Europe (though originally
from Asia) but needs some protection to
survive the winter.

Field Cricket

Gryllus campestris

ID FACT FILE

SIZE:
Body length
20–26 mm

DESCRIPTION:
Generally shiny
black, with
attractively
sculptured wings,
especially in the
male. There is a
band of yellow at
the bases of the
wings, readily
visible at rest.
There are two
long 'tails'

FOOD:
Omnivorous

LOOKALIKES:
G. bimaculatus is
very similar, but
has much longer
wings, rolled to a
point; it is
confined to south
Europe

The Field Cricket is an attractive and
distinctive creature. It favours open grassy
areas and heaths, and is particularly abundant
in lower mountain meadows where thousands
may occur in one meadow. They live in
burrows, and males sit at the entrance of these
to stridulate, producing a continuous chirping
sound; if disturbed, they retreat rapidly into
the burrow. It occurs widely in Europe except
for the extreme north, but is very rare in
Britain now, restricted to one or two
southernmost localities.

J	F	M	A	M	J
J	A	S	O	N	D

Wood Cricket
Nemobius sylvestris

ID FACT FILE

SIZE:
Body length
7–10 mm

DESCRIPTION:
A dark brown
shiny insect, with
a slender body,
long antennae,
and two long
'tails'. The
pronotum is pale
yellowish brown,
and the wings
are only about
half the length of
the abdomen

FOOD:
Mainly plant
material

LOOKALIKES:
The Marsh
Cricket
*Pteronemobius
heydenii* is
smaller and
darker; in wet
places in central-
southern Europe,
not Britain

The Wood Cricket is an inconspicuous little
insect. It lives along wood margins and in
clearings, or in more deeply shaded parts of
woods further south, where it is almost always
associated with leaf litter. In a good site,
hundreds of insects may be disturbed by
walking through, and they hop quickly away.
The call is an attractive low mellifluous
purring, easily missed if you are not 'tuned in'
to it. It is mainly a central European insect,
absent from the far north and south, and rare
in Britain, occurring only in the extreme south.

J	F	M	A	M	J
J	A	S	O	N	D

Italian or Tree Cricket
Oecanthus pellucens

ID FACT FILE

SIZE:
Body length
10–15 mm

DESCRIPTION:
Pale yellowish-brown in colour, with translucent wings. Both sexes have long antennae, but the female has two long tails in addition to the ovipositor, while the male has just two short tails

FOOD:
Mainly plant material

LOOKALIKES:
None

A very slender and rather graceful cricket, distinct from the other crickets which tend to be more robust. It is mainly active at night, moving around in trees, shrubs and tall herbage, only rarely coming to the ground. The call is a loud but quite melodious, frequently repeated note, continued for long periods. It is a warmth-loving species, occurring from south Germany and central France southwards, absent from Britain. It is most easily found by going out at night with a torch to track down the source of the calling.

most active May–Aug

Mole Cricket

Gryllotalpa gryllotalpa

ID FACT FILE

SIZE:
Body length up to 50 mm

DESCRIPTION:
A large predominantly brown insect, with broad powerful legs and a large, smooth pronotum. The wings only reach halfway down the body. There is no ovipositor

FOOD:
Mainly insect larvae

LOOKALIKES:
There are similar species in southern Europe, differing in small details. Nothing in north Europe is similar

The extraordinary Mole Crickets belong to a separate but related family, the Gryllotalpidae. In northern and central Europe, there is nothing that could be confused with it. They are burrowing insects, unable to fly or jump, and are found in damp areas where the soil is relatively soft. It is widespread in northern and central Europe from south Scandinavia southwards, though very rare in Britain. The call is a long continuous churring, not unlike that of a nightjar, though quieter and less harsh.

J	F	M	A	M	J
J	A	S	O	N	D

Common Cockroach
Blatta orientalis

ID FACT FILE

SIZE:
Body length up to 28 mm

DESCRIPTION:
A squat dark brown to blackish insect, with long antennae. Males have fully developed brownish wings (though they do not fly), while females have very short wings

FOOD:
Omnivorous, mainly carbohydrate-rich scraps

LOOKALIKES:
The American Cockroach *Periplaneta americana* is longer, with a pale brown head. Similar habitats to Common Cockroach

The Common Cockroach is a familiar pest of houses, bakeries and other warm places, despite efforts to control it. It is also known as the black beetle (though unrelated to beetles) because it resembles a fast-moving beetle. It is a native a tropical regions, but is well-established throughout much of Europe and the rest of the world, wherever conditions are favourable, though it rarely survives outdoors through the winter, except perhaps on rubbish dumps in warmer southern regions.

J	F	M	A	M	J
J	A	S	O	N	D

Dusky Cockroach
Ectobius lapponicus

ID FACT FILE

SIZE:
Body length up to about 10 mm

DESCRIPTION:
A pale greyish-brown insect, with long antennae. The pronotal disc (the hard piece that almost covers the head) is triangular with rounded corners

FOOD:
Mainly dead and decaying plant material

LOOKALIKES:
Several similar species occur, such as the more yellowish-brown Tawny Cockroach *E. pallidus* in which both sexes can fly

This slender insect is one of the native cockroaches, which, though related to the introduced species, share few of their unpleasant habitats and are certainly not pest species. In this species, males can fly well, but females have reduced wings which reach only just to the tip of the abdomen. It occurs in a variety of natural habitats such as open woods, scrub, heaths and grassland, throughout much of Europe except the far north and south. In Britain, it is uncommon and mainly southern or coastal.

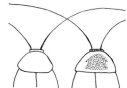

pronotal discs (which cover the thorax) of Dusky (left) and Tawny Cockroaches

J	F	M	A	M	J
J	A	S	O	N	D

Praying Mantis
Mantis religiosa

ID FACT FILE

SIZE:
Body length up to
60 mm

DESCRIPTION:
A large green
insect, with
powerful front
legs and a small
highly mobile
head. The wings
are as long as
the body, and
wholly green

FOOD:
Predatory, mainly
on insects

LOOKALIKES:
Iris oratoria looks
similar but is
smaller and has
rainbow-coloured
hindwings;
Rivetina baetica
is brown, and
females are
short-winged

In Europe, the Praying Mantis is unlikely to be
mistaken for anything else, with its distinctive
combination of size, colour and structure. It
occurs in warm, rough bushy places, being
frequent in much of southern Europe but
thinning out northwards. It can be found as far
north as north France. Its presence can often
be detected first by the egg masses – solidified
frothy creamy-brown masses containing several
hundred eggs, usually attached to plant
material. Adults can be surprisingly hard to see
despite their size.

egg mass of
Praying Mantis

EARWIGS, DERMAPTERA

J	F	M	A	M	J
J	A	S	O	N	D

Common Earwig
Forficula auricularia

ID FACT FILE

SIZE:
Body length
10–13 mm

DESCRIPTION:
A shiny brown
cylindrical insect.
Although they
appear to be
virtually
wingless, the
hindwings are
actually partly
concealed under
the modified
front wings.
Males have
pincer-like
claspers

FOOD:
Various types of
plant material

LOOKALIKES:
There are several
similar species,
but much less
common

A familiar and abundant insect, with a wealth of folk-lore and tales concerning its life history. They are much the commonest earwig in Europe, and the only species seen regularly in Britain and many other areas. They occur in a wide variety of habitats, wherever there is food and shelter, and are often found in gardens and parks, almost throughout Europe. The young are like miniature adults, and the female guards them until they disperse.

BUGS, HEMIPTERA

ID FACT FILE

SIZE:
Body length
15–17 mm

DESCRIPTION:
Generally green
in colour, with a
triangle of red on
its back (with a
green centre)
and red-tipped
wings. Antennae
relatively long,
though with few
segments

FOOD:
Leaves and fruits

LOOKALIKES:
Green Shieldbug
(p.96) is rather
similar, but all
green

Bugs divide into
two major
groups: the
heteroptera
(pp.90–118)
have the
forewings clearly
divided into a
leathery part and
a membranous
tip, while the
homopterans
(pp.119–131)
have wings with
a uniform texture

Hawthorn Shieldbug

Acanthosoma haemorrhoidale

The Hawthorn Shieldbug is one of the most
common and distinctive of the shieldbugs.
Typically, all of this group have a roughly
shield-shaped outline, though it varies in
detail. This species lives on the leaves and fruit
of shrubs and trees, especially hawthorn but
including other native deciduous species. It is
widespread over most of Europe excluding the
far north and south, and common in southern
Britain. The eggs are laid in batches of about
24 on leaves, and are large enough to be seen
with the naked eye.

Pied Shieldbug

Sehirus bicolor

ID FACT FILE

SIZE:
Body length
5–8 mm

DESCRIPTION:
An oval rather
than shield-
shaped little bug,
predominantly
black, but with
several marginal
white patches;
males and
females are
similar

FOOD:
Various parts of
its food plants

LOOKALIKES:
*Aethus
flavicornis* is
similar in size
and can be pied,
with the front
half black and
the rear white;
mainly coastal

A distinctive and attractive little bug, with an appropriate name. They occur in loose colonies on wood margins, sunny clearings and other areas of sheltered rough vegetation, where the adults live mainly on white deadnettle *Lamium album* and related *labiates*. On warm spring days, they may become mobile and fly to other locations. They are widespread in Europe except the far north; in Britain, they are largely confined to England and Wales.

BUGS, HEMIPTERA

J	F	M	A	M	J
J	A	S	O	N	D

Brassica Bug
Eurydema oleracea

ID FACT FILE

SIZE:
Body length:
5–7 mm

DESCRIPTION:
Variable in
colour, but
usually metallic
green or blue
with red, orange
or creamy spots
and patches

FOOD:
Various
members of the
cress family,
including
cabbage crops

LOOKALIKES:
E. dominulus is
similar in shape
and size, but
brighter, mainly
red with dark
markings. Similar
distribution and
food plants

A small but brightly coloured and quite
conspicuous shield bug that can often be seen
openly on plants, relying on its warning colours
to prevent predators from attacking it. They
overwinter as adults, and may appear in large
numbers in warm weather in spring. It can
become a pest on Brassica crops at times. In
Britain it is uncommon and mainly southern,
on wild members of the cress family;
throughout much of Europe it is more
frequent on both wild and cultivated species.

mating pair

BUGS, HEMIPTERA

J	F	M	A	M	J
J	A	S	O	N	D

Graphosoma italica

ID FACT FILE

Size:
Body length
10–12 mm

Description:
A boldly marked
shield-shaped
insect, with
longitudinal
unbroken stripes
the whole length
of the body. The
legs are blackish
with some red

Food:
Plant material
and products

Lookalikes:
In southern
Europe, there is
a widespread
species *G.
semipunctatum*
with the stripes
on the pronotum
broken into dots,
and the legs
all red

A very attractive and distinctive bug, with bright warning colours that indicate to potential predators that it tastes unpleasant. As a result, it tends to be found much more frequently in the open than most other shield bugs, sitting on leaves or other warm surfaces. It is a warmth-loving species, common in south Europe but increasingly rare northwards, and absent from north Europe including Britain. It occurs in a variety of rough flowery habitats, and can be frequently seen feeding on flowers.

a closely related southern
European species,
G. semipunctatum

BUGS, HEMIPTERA

| J | F | M | A | M | J |
| J | A | S | O | N | D |

Bishop's Mitre
Aelia acuminata

ID FACT FILE

Size:
Body length
8–10 mm

Description:
A narrowly oval
bug, shaped
partly like a
bishop's mitre.
It is brown with
paler brownish-
yellow patches

Food:
Grasses

Lookalikes:
None in north
Europe

A rather small shieldbug, distinctive by virtue of its shape rather than any particular colour pattern. Adults overwinter and emerge in spring to feed on various grasses, including, occasionally, cereal crops. It occurs in a variety of warm rough grassy places including roadsides, sand-dunes, heathland and woodland margins, wherever there is both food and suitable hibernation sites nearby. It is widespread on the continent, but mainly southern in Britain.

| J | F | M | A | M | J |
| J | A | S | O | N | D |

Forest Bug
Pentatoma rufipes

ID FACT FILE

SIZE:
Body length
about 15 mm

DESCRIPTION:
A dark brown
shieldbug with
(usually) a pale
orange tip to the
scutellum (in the
centre of the
back). The shape
of the pronotum,
with sharp points
on square
shoulders is
particularly
important

FOOD:
Omnivorous

LOOKALIKES:
*Picromerus
bidens* is similar,
with much longer
points to the
'shoulders'. (*see*
drawing). It is
common and
widespread

A large shieldbug, with squarish but pointed
'shoulders' to the pronotum (the exact shape is
important in distinguishing several similar
species). It occurs on and around various
deciduous trees such as oak and alder, feeding
both on the tree and on associated insects. It is
occasionally abundant in orchards, though
more as a predator than as a pest. It is
widespread almost throughout Europe except
the extreme north and south, and occurs
almost throughout Britain.

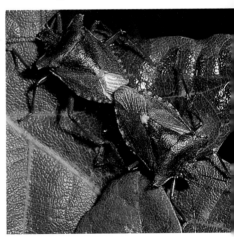

mating pair

the 'shoulders' of
Forest Bug (left) and
Picromerus bidens

BUGS, HEMIPTERA

Green Shieldbug
Palomena prasina

ID FACT FILE

Size:
Body length
12–14 mm

Description:
They are more or
less all green
when first adult
(except for the
membranous
wingtips), but
become reddish
before hiberna-
tion, re-emerging
bright green in
the spring

Food:
A wide variety of
plant material

Lookalikes:
Gorse Shieldbug
(p.98) is rather
similar, but more
slender with
reddish wings

A largish and relatively familiar shieldbug – it
is the archetypal shieldbug, shaped just like a
shield and large enough to be noticeable. It
occurs in a very wide variety of habitats,
wherever there is shelter and food, but
particularly around deciduous trees and shrubs
such as hazel and oak. Occasionally it becomes
abundant on field crops such as beans. It is
widespread throughout most of Europe, and in
Britain northwards to central Scotland, though
its range has been expanding recently.

J	F	M	A	M	J
J	A	S	O	N	D

A Shieldbug
Nezara viridula

ID FACT FILE

SIZE:
Body length
10–15 mm

DESCRIPTION:
Adults are plain
green with white
dots on the
thorax, and a
clear greenish
membrane at the
wing-tips.
Nymphs are
mainly green,
marked with
black, white
and red

LOOKALIKES:
Green Shieldbug
(p.96) is most
similar, but lacks
the white dots

Although this species does not have a
common name, it is very conspicuous and
distinctive, especially in its younger nymphal
stages (illustrated). It is widespread and often
very abundant in southern and central
Europe (but absent from Britain). It lives
in a variety of grassy and bushy places, but
becomes especially frequent in late
summer on field crops such as peas,
beans and potatoes, and it may also
become common in gardens.

nymph

J	F	M	A	M	J
J	A	S	O	N	D

Gorse Shieldbug
Piezodorus lituratus

ID FACT FILE

SIZE:
Body length
9–11 mm

DESCRIPTION:
A slender,
predominantly
green insect.
Young adults are
reddish,
especially on the
wings, but
emerge from
hibernation
bright green,
when they are
sexually mature

FOOD:
Plant material

LOOKALIKES:
Green Shieldbug
(p.96) is most
similar

A medium-sized and rather inconspicuous shieldbug. It is particularly associated with gorse, as the name suggests, but it will also occur on broom, lupins, dyer's greenweed and other related leguminous plants, so its range of habitats is very wide. In favourable conditions it becomes very abundant, and mass migrations have occasionally been recorded. It is widespread in central and southern Europe, including most of Britain, though absent from much of the far north.

J	F	M	A	M	J
J	A	S	O	N	D

Sloe Bug
Dolycoris baccarum

ID FACT FILE

SIZE:
Body length
9–12 mm

DESCRIPTION:
Typically shield-shaped, with narrow 'shoulders' that do not project beyond the width of the abdomen. They are normally brownish tinged red, and very hairy

FOOD:
A variety of plant material including fruits and seeds

LOOKALIKES:
Similar in shape to Gorse Shieldbug (p.98), but lacking the green and red pattern

A medium-sized and rather undistinguished species of shieldbug. The Sloe Bug lives mostly in association with shrubs such as sloes, hawthorn, rose and many other plants, and its most favoured habitats are woodland margins and clearings, sheltered scrub, and sand-dunes where there are suitable host plants. It is widespread and common throughout most of Europe, and much of Britain except the far north. It has a complex courtship involving large clusters of adults all together.

BUGS, HEMIPTERA

J F M A M J
J A S O N D

Squash Bug
Coreus marginatus

ID FACT FILE

SIZE:
Body length
11–13 mm

DESCRIPTION:
An all-brown
roughly shield-
shaped bug,
usually with a
slight 'waist'.
The antennae
are long and
robust, though
few-segmented

FOOD:
Leaves and fruits
of various
members of the
dock family

LOOKALIKES:
Other similar
species occur in
central and
south Europe

The squash bugs are closely related to the shieldbugs, and similar in many respects. This species is one of the largest, with particularly long antennae, which often get broken early in its life. It can occur on a wide variety of food plants, all in the dock family (including rhubarb), so it occurs in a correspondingly wide variety of habitats such as gardens, wood margins, rough pastures and elsewhere. It is widespread and abundant over much of central and southern Europe, but rare in the north. In Britain it is rare north of the Midlands.

J	F	M	A	M	J
J	A	S	O	N	D

Philomorpha laciniata

ID FACT FILE

SIZE:
Body length
9–11 mm

DESCRIPTION:
The body is
brown, strongly
indented and
very spiny – a
distinctive
combination of
features. The
antennae are
long and spiny,
particularly in the
lower half

FOOD:
Mainly plant
material of
rupturewort
(*Herniaria*) and
Paronychia

LOOKALIKES:
Nothing!

This extraordinary bug is completely
distinctive once seen, though its dull
colouring makes it difficult to spot. Adults
frequently carry a batch of large golden eggs
on their back, which have been laid there by
another female seeking to have her eggs
dispersed. They feed on a limited range of
small herbs that occur in dry grassy often
acidic slopes, particularly on sandstone and
granite, so this is their primary habitat. It is
widespread but local in central and southern
Europe, but absent from Britain.

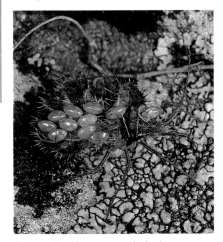

Philomorpha with ten eggs on its back

BUGS, HEMIPTERA

J	F	M	A	M	J
J	A	S	O	N	D

Alydus calcaratus

ID FACT FILE

SIZE:
Body length
about 10 mm

DESCRIPTION:
A narrowly shield-
shaped bug,
generally dark
brown in colour
when at rest, but
with a bright red
abdomen that is
exposed in flight

FOOD:
Omnivorous, on
plants, carrion
and occasionally
live prey

LOOKALIKES:
*Camptopus
lateralis* is
similar, but has
more red on the
abdomen, and
squarer pro-
notum. Central
and south
Europe only

A seemingly undistinguished bug that flashes
red when it takes off. It has one of the fastest
flights of any bug, and its colour and behaviour
can cause it to be mistaken for a Spider-hunting
Wasp. The young stages, which often occur in
ants' nests, resemble ants. Its preferred habitat
is heathland or other dry often sandy habitats
with plenty of sun. It occurs widely in central
and southern Europe, northwards into
Scandinavia; in Britain, it is much commoner in
the south, and absent from Scotland.

BUGS, HEMIPTERA

J	F	M	A	M	J
J	A	S	O	N	D

Firebug
Pyrrhocoris apterus

ID FACT FILE

SIZE:
Body length
8–11 mm

DESCRIPTION:
A squat, oval red
and black insect,
with short wings.
The head is
completely black
and there is a
large black spot
on each forewing

FOOD:
Mainly seeds
and other plant
material

LOOKALIKES:
Another bug
Corizus hyoscami
is similar but
winged, with part-
red head and
square wing
spots. Occurs in
sandy areas. *See
also Lygaeus
equestris* (p.104)

The Firebug is an attractive and conspicuous
little bug which often occurs in swarms,
especially in early spring when the adults first
emerge from their hibernation in the soil. Most
individual adults are short-winged, though a few
long-winged individuals may occur in any
population. They occur in woodland margins
and clearings, and grassy scrubby places with
bare ground and suitable hibernation sites. They
are widespread in southern and central Europe,
but very rare and wholly southern in Britain.

mass of Firebugs, adults and nymphs

a bug, *Corizus
hyoscani*, ×2

J	F	M	A	M	J
J	A	S	O	N	D

hibernates

ID FACT FILE

SIZE:
Body length
10–12 mm

DESCRIPTION:
A bright red and
black bug, with
two white spots
on the
membranous
part of the wings,
and a largely red
head

FOOD:
Fruits, seeds and
other plant
material

LOOKALIKES:
L. saxatilis has a
slightly different
pattern and no
white spots.
Similar
distribution

A Ground Bug
Lygaeus equestris

A conspicuous and attractive bug, often seen
openly on flowers or the ground – its bright
colours serve as a warning to predators that it
is poisonous or distasteful. It feeds on
developing and ripe seeds, so it can occur in a
wide variety of habitats, but particularly in
warm, sunny, well-vegetated places with
abundant flowers such as woodland margins,
amongst scrub, or in rough grassland. It is
widespread in most of Europe except for the
far north, and is absent from Britain.

the closely related
L. saxatilis

BUGS, HEMIPTERA

J	F	M	A	M	J
J	A	S	O	N	D

Red Assassin Bug
Rhinocoris iracundus

ID FACT FILE

SIZE:
Body length
14–18 mm

DESCRIPTION:
Boldly marked
with red and
black, but not as
bright as the
preceding
species, and it
can be
surprisingly
inconspicuous.
The sides of the
abdomen are
curved upwards

FOOD:
Other insects

LOOKALIKES:
R. erythropus
has the first
segment of the
beak black, not
red; *R. cuspi-
datus* has more
angular prothorax
protrusions

A large and distinctive bug, quite unlike
anything except a few closely related species.
They are predatory, and spend much time
waiting in flowers for insects, such as hoverflies
and honey bees, to alight; they seize them and
suck the contents out with their strong curved
beak. It occurs in warm, sunny flowery places
such as banks, woodland edges and scrub, and
is widespread though not abundant in central
and southern Europe. It is usually solitary, and
only one or two are seen together.

J	F	M	A	M	J
J	A	S	O	N	D

hibernates, mostly seen
Apr–June or July–Sept

ID FACT FILE

SIZE:
Body length
6–7 mm

DESCRIPTION:
A slender
brownish bug,
though very
variable in
colour, usually
with brownish
wings and an
orange-brown
abdomen. The
antennae are
long and slender

FOOD:
Predatory on
other insects

LOOKALIKES:
Marsh Damsel
Bug *Dolichonabis
limbatus* is
slightly bigger
and fatter,
always with short
wings. It is
widespread, in
damp grassland

Common Damsel Bug

Nabis rugosus

An extremely common and widespread bug,
much the commonest of the damsel bugs.
They are slender bugs, with long or short
wings, which occur in and around rough grassy
and flowery places. Adults and the oldest
nymphs are often found amongst the flowers
or the upper parts of the vegetation, while the
younger stages hunt mainly on the ground. It is
abundant throughout Europe and the British
Isles, except the extremes, wherever suitable
habitats occur.

Common Flower Bug

Anthocoris nemorum

J	F	M	A	M	J
J	A	S	O	N	D

hibernates

ID FACT FILE

Size:
Body length
4–5 mm

Description:
A slender roughly
oval insect,
generally
brownish but
with mainly
membranous
wings that have
a black spot in
the middle of
each The head is
shiny black

Food:
Various other
insects and mites

Lookalikes:
A number of
similar species,
with minor
differences, occur

A smallish bug, with distinctive shiny forewings. It is an active predator, moving rapidly when necessary to catch its prey, which it pierces with its sharp beak. Despite its small size, it can inflict a painful wound through the skin if handled. It occurs mainly in and around rough grassy flowery vegetation (though not particularly on flowers) wherever prey and hibernation sites are both available. It is particularly common on stinging nettles at times. It is widespread throughout Europe, including Britain.

Common Flower Bug, with prey

BUGS, HEMIPTERA

| J | F | M | A | M | J |
| J | A | S | O | N | D |

hibernates

ID FACT FILE

SIZE:
Body length
5–6 mm

DESCRIPTION:
A slender oval
bug, with rather
hairy wings that
have the rusty
tarnish mark and
a yellow patch
towards the tip.
The head is
usually pale
brown

FOOD:
Leaves

LOOKALIKES:
L. pratensis is
very similar,
though much
less hairy, and
with a larger
pronotum.
Common
throughout

Tarnished Plant Bug
Lygus rugulipennis

A common and widespread, though rather
inconspicuous bug, named after the rust-
coloured tarnish stain on the forewings, though
this is not always visible. It is abundant on
many sorts of plants, including wild plants such
as goosefoot, and cultivated crops such as
potatoes, lucerne and wheat. It leaves white
spots on the leaves where it has fed, though it
rarely causes serious damage. It is widespread
in most well-vegetated habitats throughout
Europe, including the British Isles.

BUGS, HEMIPTERA

Common Green Capsid

Lygocoris pabulinus

ID FACT FILE

SIZE:
Body length
7–8 mm

DESCRIPTION:
A narrowly oval
green insect,
with a distinct
'collar' behind
the head, and
pale yellowish-
brown spines on
the legs. The
membranous tips
of the wings are
brownish

FOOD:
Various
herbaceous and
woody plants

LOOKALIKES:
There are a
number of
similar species
differing in minor
details

One of a number of rather similar plant-eating
bugs that occur in a variety of habitats. It has two
distinct phases in its life, using different food
plants; the young nymphs from overwintered
eggs feed on woody plants such as hawthorn and
plum, then they transfer to a range of
herbaceous species where most of the growth
takes place. They can become quite a pest on
some crops. They are widespread throughout
most of Britain and Europe, wherever suitable
host plants and habitats occur.

BUGS, HEMIPTERA

J	F	M	A	M	J
J	A	S	O	N	D

Miris striatus

ID FACT FILE

SIZE:
Body length
10–12 mm

DESCRIPTION:
Generally black
and yellow, with
yellow and black-
striped fore-
wings, a yellow
triangle towards
the tip of each
wing before the
membranous
section, and a
yellow triangle on
the scutellum

FOOD:
Omnivorous, with
more plant
material when
young, but more
predatory when
older

LOOKALIKES:
*Calocoris
quadripunctatus*
is similar, less
boldly striped
and with a black
scutellum.
Common
throughout

This is a relatively large and conspicuous bug,
with bold markings all over. It is mainly
associated with deciduous trees and shrubs,
especially oak, hawthorn, lime, willows, hazel
and elm, where it lives amongst the foliage.
The eggs are laid in the bark of the host plant,
where they remain for the winter; in spring,
the young gradually move to the foliage to start
feeding. It is widespread and common almost
throughout Europe, including Britain, except
for the far north, in suitable wooded habitats.

*Calocoris
quadripunctatus*

BUGS, HEMIPTERA

J	F	M	A	M	J
J	A	S	O	N	D

Meadow Plant Bug
Leptoterna dolabrata

ID FACT FILE

SIZE:
Body length
9–10 mm

DESCRIPTION:
A slender bug,
with a black
head, with
yellowish or
orange wings.
The legs and
antennae are
very hairy. The
whole insect
emits a strong
smell

FOOD:
Plant material,
mainly grasses

LOOKALIKES:
L. ferrugata is
very similar,
usually more
pinkish, and it
occurs in drier
grasslands

A medium-sized plant bug, quite
conspicuously marked, but too small to be
frequently noticed. They occur, often in great
abundance, in slightly damp grassy places,
such as roadsides, meadows, water-meadows,
grassy woodland rides and so on.
Occasionally, they occur in cereal crops where
they may become a minor pest. All males are
fully winged, and can fly, but only a
proportion of females are. It is common
and widespread throughout Europe except
for the extreme north, and frequent
throughout the British Isles.

BUGS, HEMIPTERA

J	F	M	A	M	J
J	A	S	O	N	D

Water Measurer
Hydrometra stagnorum

ID FACT FILE

SIZE:
Body length
10–13 mm

DESCRIPTION:
A very slender
almost feeble-
looking insect
with long legs.
The overall
colour is dull
blackish-brown

FOOD:
Small aquatic
insects and other
invertebrates

LOOKALIKES:
Lesser Water
Measurer *H.
gracilenta* is
smaller and paler
brown. Rare in
UK, local in
Europe

A curious little insect, very easily overlooked but quite distinctive once seen. They resemble small slender stick insects, walking on the surface of the water. Their method of feeding is unusual in that they reach down through the surface of the water to spear swimming water fleas, larvae and other prey with their beak. Their preferred habitat is the sheltered well-vegetated margins of lakes and ponds, less frequently on slow-flowing waters. It is widespread and moderately common throughout almost all of Britain and Europe, except the uplands.

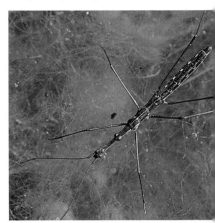

| J | F | M | A | M | J |
| J | A | S | O | N | D |

hibernates

Common Pondskater
Gerris lacustris

ID FACT FILE

SIZE:
Body length
10–12 mm

DESCRIPTION:
A long, narrow bug though quite robust in appearance. It is generally brownish or brown-grey in appearance, with a noticeably long, curved beak with which it attacks dead and stranded insects

FOOD:
Scavenges for insect remains on the surface, including anything that falls in the water

LOOKALIKES:
There are several similar species, e.g. *Aquarius najas* which is longer, always wingless, and usually in flowing water

The pondskater is a common and familiar insect almost everywhere. They are frequently to be seen out in the open, skating along on the surface of a pond or river, casting shadows where their feet rest on the surface film. This species (generally the commonest of a group of similar species) occurs in many kinds of water bodies, from chalk streams to moorland pools. Some individuals are winged, others are wingless, with all grades in between. It is common and widespread throughout most of Britain and Europe.

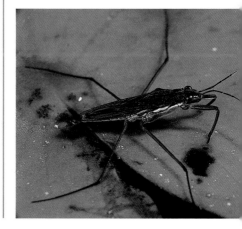

detail of long,
curved beak

J	F	M	A	M	J
J	A	S	O	N	D

Water Cricket
Velia caprai

ID FACT FILE

SIZE:
Body length
6–8 mm

DESCRIPTION:
A dark brown
insect with
orange on the
underside of the
abdomen. They
do somewhat
resemble a
cricket, but are
not related, and
no true cricket
lives on the
water surface

FOOD:
Scavenged and
live insects

LOOKALIKES:
There are rarer
closely related
species with
minor differences

Water Crickets are rather curious little insects,
though they are small and easily overlooked
thanks to their dull colouring and habit of
congregating in shady places. They often occur
in clusters on the water surface. Their
preferred habitats are still and slow-moving
waters, especially if partly shaded, in hilly
districts. The adults may be winged or virtually
wingless. They are widespread throughout
Britain and north Europe, but more local and
confined to mountain areas in the south.

BUGS, HEMIPTERA

J	F	M	A	M	J
J	A	S	O	N	D

Water Scorpion
Nepa cinerea

ID FACT FILE

SIZE:
Body length
18–24 mm,
excluding 'tail'

DESCRIPTION:
A brown insect,
with broad
flattened body
and a long hollow
'tail'. The front
pair of legs are
powerful and
enlarged

FOOD:
Predatory on
various aquatic
invertebrates

LOOKALIKES:
None

The reason for the name of this curious and very distinctive insect is immediately obvious in the body shape and the long tail, which is actually used for breathing rather than stinging. They remain semi-submerged for long periods, catching aquatic or surface-dwelling prey with their powerful front legs. It lives in still, shallow well-vegetated waters, mainly around the margins. Although some individuals can fly, they are rarely seen doing so. It is widespread through most of Britain and Europe, though rarely abundant.

the enlarged front legs of
Water Scorpion modified
for catching prey

J	F	M	A	M	J
J	A	S	O	N	D

Water Stick-insect
Ranatra linearis

ID FACT FILE

SIZE:
Body length
30–35 mm
excluding 'tail'

DESCRIPTION:
A highly
distinctive long,
thin, pale brown
insect, with a
long tail and
powerful front
legs (though
more slender
than those of
water scorpion).
The wings are
well developed,
almost as long
as the abdomen

FOOD:
Predatory on
various aquatic
creatures

LOOKALIKES:
None

The Water Stick-insect is another highly
distinctive insect from this group of water
bugs. Superficially, it does resemble a stick
insect more than the average bug, though no
European stick insect lives in an aquatic
environment. They occur in unpolluted, clear
well-vegetated still and slow-flowing waters,
such as ponds and ditches. They can fly, but
are only rarely seen to do so, most often when
their habitat becomes unsuitable. Widespread
in southern and central Europe, and in the
southern half of Britain.

BUGS, HEMIPTERA

J	F	M	A	M	J
J	A	S	O	N	D

Common Backswimmer

Notonecta glauca

ID FACT FILE

SIZE:
Body length
about 15 mm

DESCRIPTION:
A greyish-brown
insect that
normally looks
silvery because
of its air bubble
and the silvery
forewings. Its
back legs are
strongly
developed for
swimming

FOOD:
Various aquatic
animals including
tadpoles and
small fish

LOOKALIKES:
There are several
similar species
with small
differences

This intriguing bug is also known as the Water
Boatman, and its two names come from its
habit of swimming on its back, with a large
bubble of water attached to its belly and its
broad legs looking like oars. It is a highly active
species, with fully developed wings, and will
quite readily fly to seek out new habitats and
food sources. The adults are predatory, with a
powerful bite that can easily pierce human
skin. It is frequent in various types of still and
slow-moving water throughout most of Britain
and Europe.

BUGS, HEMIPTERA

| J | F | M | A | M | J |
| J | A | S | O | N | D |

Lesser Water Boatman
Corixa punctata

ID FACT FILE

SIZE:
Body length
6–8 mm

DESCRIPTION:
A narrowly oval
insect, generally
brown to
brownish-yellow
in colour. The
wings and
pronotum are
striped
transversely with
black and white
bands

FOOD:
Mostly living or
dead plant
material

LOOKALIKES:
There are several
similar species,
often
distinguishable
only by
microscopic
examination

This is actually one of several similar species known by this common name. Unlike the Common Backswimmer (p.117), they swim the right way up in the water and do not have such markedly developed hind legs. When courting, males 'sing' quite audibly by rubbing bristly patches on their front legs against their head. They occur in clean but well-vegetated ponds, ditches, and slow-flowing rivers, which may be slightly brackish. They are widespread virtually throughout Europe in suitable habitats.

J	F	M	A	M	J
J	A	S	O	N	D

ID FACT FILE

SIZE:
Body length
30–37 mm

DESCRIPTION:
A bulky brownish
insect, with
transparent
brown-veined
wings. The call is
a loud piercing
continuous
noise, audible
from a
considerable
distance

FOOD:
They suck sap
from plants

LOOKALIKES:
There are many
other cicadas in
southern Europe,
with small
differences.
Cicada orni is
distinctive by the
eleven dark
spots on each
forewing

Cicada
Tibicen plebejus

The Cicadas are a distinctive and well-known
group, famous for their loud continuous calls,
though actually rarely seen unless searched for.
They are most often seen on or near to the
trunk or branches of their tree. This is the
largest of the European cicadas, a very bulky
insect with a particularly loud and penetrating
call. It occurs in and around trees and open
woodland, especially of pines (and particularly
umbrella pines) throughout southern Europe,
but not extending far north.

BUGS, HEMIPTERA

| J | F | M | A | M | J |
| J | A | S | O | N | D |

'New Forest Cicada'
Cicadetta montana

ID FACT FILE

SIZE:
Body length
16–20 mm

DESCRIPTION:
A small cicada,
generally
brownish-orange,
with the
abdomen banded
with orange. The
wings are clear,
with orange-
brown veins
towards the edge

FOOD:
Plant sap

LOOKALIKES:
There are several
similar species
in C/S Europe.
C. argentata is
most similar, but
with red on the
pronotum.
Similar habitats,
not UK

In Britain, this is known as the New Forest
Cicada because this is the only place in Britain
where it occurs, in very small numbers. It is
more frequent in central and southern Europe,
though absent from the north. Its preferred
habitat is woodland clearings and margins, and
is frequently associated with lime trees and
walnuts. Its call is a more gentle purring
warble, much less noticeable than larger
cicadas. The young stages, as with other
cicadas, live underground for several years,
feeding on plants.

| J | F | M | A | M | J |
| J | A | S | O | N | D |

Horned Treehopper
Centrotus cornutus

ID FACT FILE

SIZE:
Body length
6–7 mm

DESCRIPTION:
A squat brown insect, with brown body and brown-tinted wings; the pronotum extending down the back is brown, leathery and downy, with pointed projections on the shoulders

FOOD:
Plant sap

LOOKALIKES:
A smaller species *Gargara genistae*, with a shorter pronotum, occurs on broom and gorse

A curiously shaped little insect, easily recognised once known, though rather small and inconspicuous. They have a hunched squarish shape, with long pointed projections from the 'shoulders' – part of the long, leathery pronotum that extends all down the back. Their main habitat is woodland rides, clearings and margins, and other sheltered flowery places, where they are most likely to be found attached to the stems. They are locally common throughout most of Britain and Europe.

BUGS, HEMIPTERA

| J | F | M | A | M | J |
| J | A | S | O | N | D |

Buffalo Treehopper
Stictocephalus bisonia

ID FACT FILE

SIZE:
Body length
6–8 mm

DESCRIPTION:
A squat hunched
insect, almost
wholly green in
colour except for
variable reddish
lines on the
pronotum. The
wings are clear
but tinted
greenish

FOOD:
Plant sap

LOOKALIKES:
None

The Buffalo Treehopper is an interesting and distinctive insect, so called because of its hunched shoulders and bison-like shape. The shape is due mainly to a large extended pronotum that covers most of the body. It comes originally from North America, but has become established locally in Europe in wooded habitats and orchards, where it may cause some damage. In Britain, it rarely persists for long. If disturbed, they can jump or fly to escape, though they tend to just move out sight.

Buffalo Treehopper,
front view

J	F	M	A	M	J
J	A	S	O	N	D

Cercopis vulnerata

ID FACT FILE

SIZE:
Body length
9–12 mm

DESCRIPTION:
A boldly marked
insect, shiny
black with five
extensive red
patches visible
from above. The
antennae are
very short

FOOD:
Various herbs
and shrubs

LOOKALIKES:
There are no
similar species
in the UK, but in
south Europe
C. arcuata has
smaller red
patches, with the
rear one reduced
to a straight line

It is surprising that this distinctive little
froghopper does not have an English name, as
it is easily recognisable and clearly visible,
although small. True to its name, the adults
hop readily away from danger, though they
make little attempt at concealment thanks to
their warning colours. It is frequent in warm
bushy and rough grassy places, such as scrub
and woodland margins. In Britain, it is only
common in the south, but it is more
widespread in continental Europe. The
nymphs live communally on roots, protected
by hardened froth.

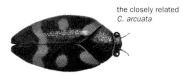

the closely related
C. arcuata

J	F	M	A	M	J
J	A	S	O	N	D

Common Froghopper
Philaenus spumarius

Although the adult Common Froghoppers are not very well-known, their young nymph stages are much more familiar – the mass of frothy white liquid around them is the familiar 'cuckoo spit' of spring and early summer. The older insects emerge from the froth to live amongst soft herbaceous plants, on which they feed. They can occur in a wide variety of well-vegetated sheltered habitats, including gardens, and they are abundant throughout most of Britain and Europe.

ID FACT FILE

Size:
Body length
5–6 mm

Description:
Nymphs are yellowish brown to greenish; adults variable, brownish-yellow with different patterns of darker and lighter, though usually the head is pale

Food:
Plant sap

Lookalikes:
There are several similar species, such as the larger *Aphrophora alni* with a keeled pronotum. Common and widespread

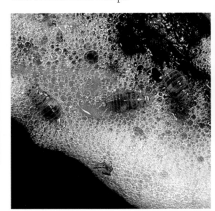

Common Froghopper nymphs

adult Common
Froghopper ×3

BUGS, HEMIPTERA

Cicadella viridis

ID FACT FILE

SIZE:
Body length
7–9 mm

DESCRIPTION:
The most noticeable feature is the strongly coloured wings, which are green or blue-green (males are darker) with a similar-coloured pronotum and a greenish-yellow head. The yellowish hind legs are spiny

FOOD:
Grasses

LOOKALIKES:
None

A distinctive and conspicuous little leafhopper (the leafhoppers can be distinguished from the froghoppers by their distinctly spiny back legs). It is one of the larger leafhoppers, and since it often occurs in abundance, it can be very noticeable. They occur mainly in damper lush grassy places such as wet meadows, marshes and bogs. They hop readily and openly if disturbed. Widespread and abundant in suitable habitats throughout most of Britain and Europe.

BUGS, HEMIPTERA

Rhododendron Leafhopper

Graphocephala fennahi

| J | F | M | A | M | J |
| J | A | S | O | N | D |

ID FACT FILE

SIZE:
Body length
8–10 mm

DESCRIPTION:
A greenish
insect, similar in
general shape to
other leaf-
hoppers, but with
several pairs of
clear red stripes
on the wings
forming V shapes
over the back

FOOD:
Rhododendrons

LOOKALIKES:
None

This is a wholly distinctive little leafhopper. It was originally introduced from North America with plant material, but has become established – and is still spreading – in southern Britain and perhaps elsewhere. The eggs are laid in the developing flower buds of Rhododendrons in autumn, and they hatch the following spring. It occurs wherever there are suitable rhododendron bushes, both in gardens and parks, and where they have become naturalised in the wild such as heaths and woods.

BUGS, HEMIPTERA

Woolly Aphid
Eriosoma lanigerum

ID FACT FILE

SIZE:
Body length
2–3 mm
individually

DESCRIPTION:
The adults are
brown or black,
clothed with waxy
fluff; winged or
wingless. The
waxy patches
clothing the
young aphids are
most noticeable

FOOD:
Plant sap

LOOKALIKES:
None

An all-too-familiar insect, particularly in its young stages. The young aphids are surrounded and protected by masses of white fluffy waxy material, which prevents predators from seeing or reaching them, and which also protects against pesticide sprays. They occur on a variety of trees and shrubs, especially apples, and the colonies may be found on the bark particularly around cracks or wounds. Some of the adults are winged, allowing dispersal to new sites.

Woolly Aphids on Cotoneaster

Black Bean Aphid
Aphis fabae

ID FACT FILE

SIZE:
Body length
2 mm

DESCRIPTION:
A small black or
greenish-black
aphid, with long
antennae but
short rear
projections
(cornicles). They
may be winged or
wingless

FOOD:
The sap of
various plants,
mainly
herbaceous

LOOKALIKES:
There are several
similar species

Another all-too-familiar aphid, often just
referred to as 'blackfly' when it colonises the
tips of broad beans in abundance. In fact, it has
a more complex life-cycle: in autumn, winged
females from the summer herbaceous host
migrate to woody plants such as spindle to lay
eggs which hatch into wingless females. These
mate, lay eggs and die. The following spring
the eggs hatch into females which produce live
young without mating. These then return to
infest the herbaceous plants. It is a widespread
and abundant species.

adult Black Bean
Aphid ×10

Rose Aphid
Macrosiphum rosae

ID FACT FILE

SIZE:
Body length up to 3 mm

DESCRIPTION:
A relatively large plump aphid, green or red in general colour, with two long black projections (cornicles) at the rear end

FOOD:
The sap of plants

LOOKALIKES:
There are several similar species, though the long cornicles are a useful identification guide

This largish aphid is the one most frequently known to gardeners as 'greenfly', though in fact there are as many pink individuals as green ones in most colonies. It has a complex life-cycle like many other aphids, and occurs on roses (usually on stems below flower buds) in abundance in spring, transferring later in summer to other herbaceous species such as teasels. There are winged and wingless individuals in colonies. It is widespread and abundant throughout Britain and Europe.

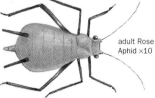

adult Rose Aphid ×10

J	F	M	A	M	J
J	A	S	O	N	D

Cabbage Whitefly
Aleyrodes proletella

These tiny active little insects most resemble small moths, are called 'flies', but are actually true bugs! Although individually small, they are often conspicuous by their abundance, especially in late summer. This species attacks cultivated brassicas and relatives, occurring mainly on the undersides of the leaves where they cause discoloring. It is common and widespread throughout most of Britain and Europe wherever suitable food plants occur. They are also known as 'snowy fly'.

ID FACT FILE

SIZE:
Body length
2–3 mm

DESCRIPTION:
Almost entirely white, with waxy white wings and even white legs and antennae. The wings are broad, and held flat like a moth at rest

FOOD:
The sap of cabbages and their relatives

LOOKALIKES:
The greenhouse whitefly *Trileurodes vaporariorum* is not so brightly white. It only survives for long in greenhouses

BUGS, HEMIPTERA

J	F	M	A	M	J
J	A	S	O	N	D

Mussel Scale

Lepidosaphes ulmi

ID FACT FILE

SIZE:
Body length
3–5 mm long

DESCRIPTION:
The scales under
which the insects
hide are brown
and curved,
resembling tiny
mussels. They
occur in groups
on the bark of
trees

FOOD:
The sap of trees

LOOKALIKES:
There are several
similar species;
*Parthenole-
canium corni* has
rounded
hemispherical
scales, in similar
places

Scale insects bear little resemblance to other
bugs superficially, as they cover themselves with
a protective scale-like secretion, giving them the
appearance of tiny molluscs (in this case,
mussels). Under each scale is a female who lays
her eggs then dies, and the tiny nymphs hatch
out about a month later, to spread out and find
new feeding sites. Males, which only form a
small part of the population, are winged and
active. They are widespread and common
throughout on deciduous trees, especially apple.

THRIPS, THYSANOPTERA

| J | F | M | A | M | J |
| J | A | S | O | N | D |

Pea Thrips
Kakothrips pisivorus

ID FACT FILE

SIZE:
Body length:
approx. 2 mm

DESCRIPTION:
A narrowly
cylindrical dark
brown insect,
with thin feathery
wings that reach
about two-thirds
of the way down
the abdomen.
The legs are
partly yellow

FOOD:
The flowers and
young fruit of
legumes
including peas

LOOKALIKES:
There are many
similar species,
needing
microscopic
examination to
separate them

Thrips are mostly tiny inconspicuous insects,
though there are several hundred species in
Europe. They include the familiar thunder flies
which occur in such abundance on thundery
August days. They all have distinctive feathery
wings, usually with two pairs. This species lives
in the flowers of peas and other legumes,
causing damage to the developing pods. It is
widespread and abundant in Britain and
Europe, occasionally becoming a pest on crops.

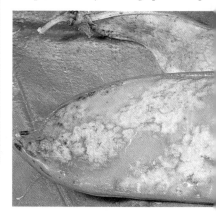

Pea Thrips damage to pea pod

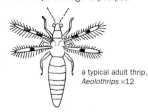

a typical adult thrip,
Aeolothrips ×12

| J | F | M | A | M | J |
| J | A | S | O | N | D |

Cat Flea
Ctenocephalides felis

ID FACT FILE

SIZE:
Body length
3–4 mm

DESCRIPTION:
Dark brown
slender insects,
flattened in one
plane, and very
robust. This
species has a
long narrow
head, and
particularly spiny
legs

FOOD:
The blood of
their host

LOOKALIKES:
There are several
similar species;
dog fleas *C.
canis* are slightly
larger with a
rounder head,
and they occur
on dogs

The Cat Flea is typical of a number of species occurring on different hosts. They are wingless, jumping, blood-sucking insects which live in close proximity with their host – in this case, the cat. The females lay pearly white eggs on the host and nearby bedding, and the worm-like larvae feed on detritus and pupate in cocoons. They are stimulated to emerge as adults by movement and warmth, so they may remain dormant for long periods when no mammals are present. They are widespread and common almost everywhere.

adult flea

eggs and larvae
of Cat Flea ×6

J	F	M	A	M	J
J	A	S	O	N	D

An Ant-lion
Euroleon nostras

ID FACT FILE

SIZE:
Body length about 25–30 mm

DESCRIPTION:
A delicate, long, thin insect, with finely veined slightly spotted translucent wings. The body is brownish-grey. The antennae are much longer than those of a damselfly

FOOD:
Predatory on other insects

LOOKALIKES:
There are several similar species, such as *Myrmeleon formicarius* which has lightly spotted wings, and slightly clubbed antennae. Similar habitats, though often in drier more open sites

The ant-lions are a distinctive group of insects, mainly found in the warmer parts of the world, but with a few species in Europe. The larvae live in the ground, where they sit at the base of a crater; small insects – such as ants – fall into the crater and become stuck, assisted by the larva throwing up soil to land on it. They are then eaten. The adults can fly, and bear some resemblance to a delicate damselfly. This is one of the most widespread European species, occurring from south Sweden southwards in dry but shady places such as open woodland. Recently discovered in eastern England.

J	F	M	A	M	J
J	A	S	O	N	D

An Ascalaphid
Libelloides coccajus

ID FACT FILE

SIZE:
Body length
19–21 mm

DESCRIPTION:
The body is black
and furry, with
curved claspers
at the rear in
males. The wings
are translucent,
heavily veined,
suffused with
large yellow
patches and
black towards
the base

FOOD:
Other insects

LOOKALIKES:
There are several
similar species
in south Europe,
such as *L.
longicornis* which
has yellow veins
on the forewing

The ascalaphids are a small group of highly
distinctive insects, related to ant-lions but
looking superficially like dragonflies. The long
heavily clubbed antennae are a key feature.
They are sun-loving insects, frequently settling
with wings open to bask but closing them in
dull weather. They are predatory on other
insects, catching them in flight. This species
occurs commonly in sunny grassy glades, wood
margins and rough flowery places in south and
central Europe, excluding Britain.

J	F	M	A	M	J
J	A	S	O	N	D

Giant Lacewing

Osmylus fulvicephalus

ID FACT FILE

SIZE:
Body length
20–30 mm

DESCRIPTION:
The body is
slender and
brownish, but it
is wholly hidden
by the large net-
veined dark-
spotted wings
that are held
tent-like over the
body when at
rest

FOOD:
Other insects

LOOKALIKES:
None

This is one of the largest of the lacewings,
though surprisingly easily overlooked as it feeds
mainly at night and hides under bridges and
fallen tree trunks during the day. The adults,
though carnivorous, are quite slow-moving and
may even visit flowers – most of the feeding is
done in the larval stages. Its preferred habitat is
woodlands with flowing water, though it can be
found in other damp shady places. It is
widespread in Europe except for the north, and
in Britain it is local and southern.

J	F	M	A	M	J
J	A	S	O	N	D

Green Lacewing

Chrysopa perla

ID FACT FILE

SIZE:
Body length
10–15 mm, or
18–20 mm to
folded wingtips

DESCRIPTION:
The body is pale
green marked
with black as is
the head. The
wings are
membranous,
slightly bluish-
green, with some
black cross-
veins. The
antennae are
long and fine

FOOD:
Insects

LOOKALIKES:
C. carnea is very
similar, with a
pale green
unmarked body
and clear green
wings. Similar
habitats

One of several rather similar species known
collectively as green lacewings. They are a
distinctive and attractive group of delicate
slow-moving insects, which often come into
houses in autumn, attracted by the light.
Their larvae are voracious predators, and are
especially fond of aphids, so they should be
welcome in every garden. This particular
species mainly occurs in woodland or
well-treed gardens and parks, and is
widespread throughout Europe except
the far north. In Britain, it is mainly
southern in distribution.

J	F	M	A	M	J
J	A	S	O	N	D

A Brown Lacewing

Hemerobius lutescens

ID FACT FILE

SIZE:
Body length
7–10 mm

DESCRIPTION:
The body is
brown and
cylindrical, and
the translucent
pale brown wings
have dark spots

FOOD:
Other insects,
especially aphids

LOOKALIKES:
There are many
similar species

In general, the brown lacewings are an inconspicuous group of insects. They are small, brownish-grey in colour, and mainly nocturnal. Like the green lacewings, they are predatory, especially on aphids. The wings are held roof-wise over the body, and the antennae are relatively long. This particular species is one of a number of similar species, distinguishable only by detailed examination of wing patterns. It is frequent and widespread throughout most of Europe, rarest in the south, in lightly wooded areas, parks, and woodland margins, particularly where oaks are present.

J	F	M	A	M	J
J	A	S	O	N	D

Alder Fly
Sialis lutaria

ID FACT FILE

SIZE:
Body length
18–22 mm

DESCRIPTION:
The most
distinctive
feature is the
smoky brown
wings with few,
thick veins, held
tent-like over the
body. It is a dark
brown insect
overall

FOOD:
The larvae are
voracious
predators; adults
feed a little,
mainly on pollen

LOOKALIKES:
There are several
similar species
in north Europe

Alder Flies, though neither large nor brightly
coloured, are quite often noticed because they
perch on leaves, trunks and other objects, and
tend not to fly away. The larvae are aquatic,
and so the adults are most frequently found
near water, especially in wooded areas. There
is no specific association with alders, except
that alders are often present in waterside
woodland. They are widespread throughout
north and central Europe, though confined to
mountains further south. In Britain, they are
common and widespread.

J	F	M	A	M	J
J	A	S	O	N	D

A Snake Fly
Raphidia maculicollis

ID FACT FILE

SIZE:
Body length
15–18 mm

DESCRIPTION:
The body is
slender,
cylindrical and
dark brown, with
a long 'neck'
forward of where
the wings are
inserted. The
wings are clear,
though with well-
marked veins

FOOD:
Other insects

LOOKALIKES:
There are similar
species, e.g. *R.
notata*, which has
a slightly broader
head, and is
associated with
oaks

Snake flies as a group (family Raphidiidae) are
easily identified by their long, slightly snake-like
neck, with the head often held slightly above the
body. They are slow-moving but predatory
insects, seen on bark and leaves. The preferred
habitat of this species is coniferous woodland,
though it occasionally occurs in other wooded
places. Males and females differ only in the long
bristle-like ovipositor of the females. It is
widespread in Europe except for the far south
and north, and frequent throughout Britain.

Scorpion Fly
Panorpa communis

ID FACT FILE

SIZE:
Body length
17–20 mm

DESCRIPTION:
A distinctive
group of insects,
with a long
robust downward-
pointed 'beak',
and the male's
upturned tail.
The wings are
spotted with
black, and the
body is yellowish

FOOD:
Dead and dying
insects and
invertebrates

LOOKALIKES:
There are about
30 species in
Europe differing
in minor details

Scorpion flies are so-called because the males
have an upturned and curled over sting-like
tail, resembling a scorpion, though they are
quite harmless. They live as scavengers, or
weak predators, including the skilful removal
of prey from spiders' webs without themselves
getting caught. Their preferred habitat is
woodland, hedgerows and other places with
trees and shade. This particular species is very
widespread throughout most of Europe,
including most of Britain.

the Scorpion Fly's
specialised 'beak'

J	F	M	A	M	J
J	A	S	O	N	D

A Caddis Fly

Phryganea grandis

ID FACT FILE

SIZE:
Body length
20–30 mm

DESCRIPTION:
A moth-like
insect, with
wings folded
roof-wise along
the length of the
body. The larger
females have a
pattern of black
marks on the
wing. The
antennae are
long, and the
legs have several
robust spines

FOOD:
Adults rarely feed

LOOKALIKES:
The most similar
species is *P.
striata*, where
the female has a
thinner wing
stripe broken
into three
dashes

This species is the largest of British caddis
flies, and one of the largest in Europe. It is
known as the 'great red sedge' amongst
fishermen. Caddis flies are intermediate in
appearance between moths and flies,
resembling each in some respects. The larvae
of this species live in still or slow-moving
water, including larger rivers, making typical
caddis cases using plant fragments. The adults
are usually found in damp habitats nearby.
They are widespread throughout Britain and
most of Europe except the far south.

J	F	M	A	M	J
J	A	S	O	N	D

Philopotamus montanus

ID FACT FILE

Size:
Body length
12 mm

Description:
A small
essentially
brownish insect,
with mottled
yellow and brown
forewings, and
greyish
hindwings. At
rest, it adopts
the typical
caddis-fly
posture with the
wings held like a
tent

Food:
Algae, detritus
etc.

Lookalikes:
Distinctive in
Britain, though
similar species
occur in north
Europe

This attractive little insect is one of the most
distinctive of the caddis flies, with its colourful
patterned wings. The larvae live mainly in fast-
flowing streams in hill and mountain areas,
where they spin nets in the form of long
tubular bags on the undersides of rocks, to
catch diatoms and detritus. The adults do not
move far, and are most likely to be found
around mountain streams. It is widespread
throughout most of central and northern
Europe in suitable areas, but is rather
uncommon and mainly western in Britain.

J	F	M	A	M	J
J	A	S	O	N	D

Rhyacophila sp

ID FACT FILE

SIZE:
Body length
9–11 mm

DESCRIPTION:
A brownish-yellow
insect, with
clear, shiny, well-
veined wings.
The antennae
are shorter and
more robust than
those of many
caddis flies, and
the wings are
less hairy

FOOD:
Predatory larvae,
feeds little as
adult

LOOKALIKES:
There are several
similar species;
R. obliterata is
most distinctive,
with bright yellow
wings when
newly emerged

An attractive, though inconspicuous caddis fly which is one of a small group of similar species favouring flowing, clean, often upland streams. The larvae are unusual amongst caddis flies in that they do not construct a protective case of plants or stones, and move freely on the stream bed as predators on other invertebrates. The adults are mainly active at night, and will fly to nearby lights. They are widespread in Britain and much of Europe, though confined to mountain areas further south.

TRUE FLIES, DIPTERA

Giant Cranefly
Tipula maxima

ID FACT FILE

SIZE:
Body length
28–32 mm

DESCRIPTION:
The body is
brownish, with a
blunt abdomen in
males, pointed in
females. The
large wings are
heavily marked
with dark
patches
occupying about
half of the area

FOOD:
The larvae live on
the roots of
aquatic plants;
the adults rarely
feed

LOOKALIKES:
T. vittata is the
most similar, but
smaller with less
extensive wing
markings.
Widespread

A large and distinctive cranefly, easily
distinguished from the run-of-the-mill 'daddy
long-legs' craneflies, by its larger size and
boldly marked wings. When settled, it holds its
wings wide open, almost like a dragonfly. The
larvae live in mud around ponds and slow-
moving streams, and the adults are likely to be
found nearby in damp woods, wet heathy
areas, and water-meadows. It is widespread
throughout most of Britain and Europe,
especially in upland areas.

TRUE FLIES, DIPTERA

| J | F | M | A | M | J |
| J | A | S | O | N | D |

Cranefly
Tipula paludosa

This is one of several common closely related species known commonly as 'daddy long-legs'. They are particularly abundant in late summer and autumn, when they are attracted to lights and often enter houses in large numbers. The larvae are known as 'leatherjackets' due to their tough skins, and they feed underground where they can do some damage to plants. They are most frequent in and around permanent pastures and other grassy areas, and are widespread throughout most of Britain and Europe.

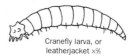

Cranefly larva, or
leatherjacket ×⅔

TRUE FLIES, DIPTERA

J	F	M	A	M	J
J	A	S	O	N	D

Spotted Cranefly
Nephrotoma appendiculata

ID FACT FILE

SIZE:
Body length
18–24 mm

DESCRIPTION:
Similar in form to
other craneflies,
but with a yellow
body marked
with black,
especially on the
thorax and
abdomen. The
female has a
pointed red tip to
the abdomen

FOOD:
The larvae feed
on the roots of
plants

LOOKALIKES:
N. crocata has a
more boldly
marked
abdomen, black
with yellow rings

Although similar in general form to the
commoner 'daddy long-legs', the Spotted
Cranefly is much more distinctively marked, and
can be readily recognised. It is common and
widespread, and can occur in a variety of habitats
such as woods, old pastures, roadside verges,
parks and gardens, though it is much less likely
to enter houses than the daddy long-legs. It
occurs throughout Britain, and most of Europe.
The larvae are known as leatherjackets, though
they are rarely as damaging as the *Tipula* larvae.

the closely related
N. crocata ×1½

TRUE FLIES, DIPTERA

J	F	M	A	M	J
J	A	S	O	N	D

Ctenophora ornata

ID FACT FILE

SIZE:
Body length
15–20 mm

DESCRIPTION:
The thorax and
abdomen are
bright yellow with
black bands and
an orange tip.
The males have
large feathery
antennae, while
the females have
a pointed
abdomen

FOOD:
Feeds mainly in
larval stage, on
rotting wood

LOOKALIKES:
C. atrata is
darker, with
smaller
antennae.
Similar habitats

This cranefly is a very attractive and highly
distinctive insect, with its brightly coloured
body, large feathery antennae (in the male)
and dark spot on the wing. Unlike the more
common and widespread craneflies, the
larvae of this one live in decaying timber such
as old tree trunks, usually in shady situations.
The most likely habitat is old deciduous
woodland with ancient trees. It is rare and
local in Britain, but more widespread and
frequent in Europe, especially in well-wooded
hilly areas.

TRUE FLIES, DIPTERA

J	F	M	A	M	J
J	A	S	O	N	D

A Mosquito
Culex pipiens

ID FACT FILE

SIZE:
Body length
5–7 mm

DESCRIPTION:
A smallish
mosquito, with
grey-brown body,
and white bands
on each
abdominal
segment

FOOD:
Mammalian
blood

LOOKALIKES:
There are several
similar species;
*Culiseta
annulata* is even
more boldly
banded, but
larger

Mosquitoes are all-too-familiar as small
whining flies which attack and suck blood,
particularly at night or in dull weather. In fact,
it is only the female which does this, requiring
blood before the eggs can be laid. The males
have feathery antennae, and hairy palps
between the antennae. This is one of the
commonest mosquitoes, though one of the
least likely to bite, and it occurs everywhere;
although the larvae live in water, almost any
water will do, including a puddle. It occurs
throughout Europe.

TRUE FLIES, DIPTERA

St Mark's Fly

Bibio marci

ID FACT FILE

Size:
Body length
about 10 mm

Description:
The body and
head are black
and furry. The
legs are black
and robust, and
the wings are
completely clear

Food:
Feeds mainly in
the larval stage,
though nectar is
taken by the
adults

Lookalikes:
B. hortulanus is
similar in shape,
but females are
orange-red, and
less hairy.
Widespread

The St. Mark's Fly is the only insect from this
family that is at all familiar to the general
public. It is known as the St. Mark's Fly
because it appears at or about St. Mark's day,
at the end of April. The flies settle on
vegetation and flowers, and fly off slowly,
trailing their legs, if disturbed. Their favoured
habitats include woodland margins, grassy
roadsides, hedgebanks, especially where
flowering hawthorn trees are present. It is
common throughout Britain and most of
central and north Europe.

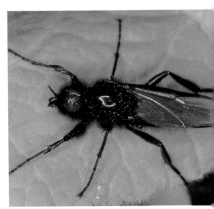

TRUE FLIES, DIPTERA

Speedwell Gall
Jaapiella veronicae

ID FACT FILE

SIZE:
Body length
2–3 mm

DESCRIPTION:
The body is
narrow and
triangular,
yellowish. The
wings are fringed
with hairs, and
the antennae are
like fine strings
of pearls with
whorls of hairs
(lens needed)

FOOD:
Speedwells

LOOKALIKES:
None

The adult flies of this species are not
generally known, but the galls that they
cause are quite familiar. The buds of
speedwells, especially bird's eye (germander)
speedwell, become swollen like little hairy
spheres when the larvae of the fly are
developing in them. The adults emerge, and
may swarm to lights on summer evenings. It is
widespread and common, wherever suitable
speedwells occur such as in flowery old
grassland and woodland rides. It occurs
throughout Britain and most of Europe.

galls on Germander
Speedwell

the adult gall-
causing fly ×6

J	F	M	A	M	J
J	A	S	O	N	D

TRUE FLIES, DIPTERA

J	F	M	A	M	J
J	A	S	O	N	D

A Soldier Fly
Stratiomys chameleon

ID FACT FILE

SIZE:
Body length
8–11 mm

DESCRIPTION:
A boldly marked
insect, with black
thorax, and
yellow and black-
striped
abdomen. The
wings are
narrower than
the body when at
rest, and the
antennae are
relatively long

FOOD:
Adults visit
flowers for nectar

LOOKALIKES:
S. potamida is
similar, but with
smaller areas of
yellow and thin
uninterrupted
lower abdomen
bands

This species is one of the largest and most
conspicuous of a group of flies known
collectively as soldier flies on account of their
bright colours. They resemble some hoverflies,
but have more flattened bodies and longer
antennae. The larvae are aquatic, though in
some species they may emerge and travel
overland to find pupation sites. The adults are
most frequent in marshy wetland areas, where
there is some open water, and they often visit
flowers. They are mainly southern, and
uncommon, in the UK but more frequent and
widespread in Europe.

TRUE FLIES, DIPTERA

Snipe Fly
Rhagio scolopacea

ID FACT FILE

SIZE:
Body length
10–12 mm

DESCRIPTION:
A dull, rather
inconspicuous
fly, with a
brownish-black
abdomen banded
with yellow
(though this is
barely noticeable
when the wings
are closed). The
wings are
transparent but
with darker spots

FOOD:
Larvae
carnivorous,
adults rarely
seen feeding

LOOKALIKES:
R. tringaria is
very similar, but
with unspotted
wings

A rather distinctive fly, once learnt, though
often confused with biting insects such as
mosquitoes by the general public. When
resting, they almost invariably perch on a
vertical surface such as a wall or tree trunk,
with the head pointing downwards, which helps
to distinguish them. They occur in damp grassy
and lightly wooded places, and the larvae live
carnivorously in damp soil. It is common and
widespread in both Britain and Europe, and
may become abundant in favoured habitats.

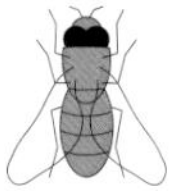

J	F	M	A	M	J
J	A	S	O	N	D

A Horsefly

Tabanus sudeticus

ID FACT FILE

SIZE:
Body length 20–25 mm

DESCRIPTION:
A robust squat insect, with strong piercing mouthparts (in females). The abdomen varies in colour, mainly brownish-black with yellow triangles on each segment

FOOD:
Females drink mammalian blood, males visit flowers for nectar

LOOKALIKES:
Several species are similar. *T. bovinus* is the closest, usually more orange-brown, with longer triangles

There are a number of similar horseflies, of which this is one of the largest. The females suck the blood of mammals, inflicting a painful wound, though they are so large that one normally hears them coming. As the name suggests, they occur around horses and other mammals. The larvae live in damp soil, and the adults are most likely to be found in damp pastures where there are grazing animals regularly. It is common and widespread throughout most of Europe, especially in upland areas.

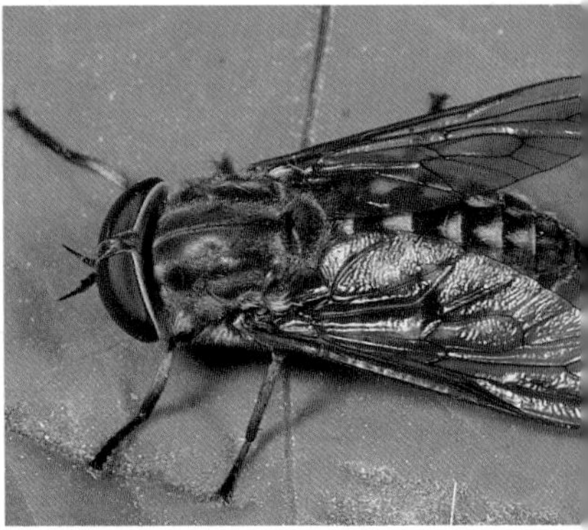

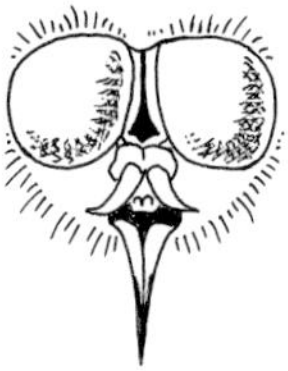

mouthparts of female horsefly ×3

J	F	M	A	M	J
J	A	S	O	N	D

Cleg
Haematopota pluvialis

ID FACT FILE

SIZE:
Body length
10–12 mm

DESCRIPTION:
Predominantly
greyish, though
on close inspec-
tion, the combi-
nation of mottled
wings and irides-
cent greenish
eyes is quite
attractive. The
wings are closed
over the body at
rest, not held in
a triangle like the
Chrysops species
(p.156)

FOOD:
Females suck
the blood of
mammals

LOOKALIKES:
There are several
very similar
species, hard
to distinguish
in the field

The little Cleg – a close relative of the horse
flies – is one of the most universally disliked
of insects! The females approach quietly and
inconspicuously, and often the first sign of
their presence is the sharp pain as they bite.
The bites will continue to 'itch' for several days
afterwards. As with horseflies, the males do not
bite. The larvae live in damp soil, and the
adults are most likely to be found in damp
grassy areas, especially pastures, where they
may become abundant. They are all-too-
widespread, throughout Britain and Europe.

TRUE FLIES, DIPTERA

J	F	M	A	M	J
J	A	S	O	N	D

Chrysops relictus

ID FACT FILE

SIZE:
Body length
10 mm

DESCRIPTION:
The abdomen is
broad, yellowish
with black
markings
towards the
front, black in
the rear half. The
wings are partly
clear with dark
markings, and
the eyes are
bright iridescent
green

FOOD:
Females drink
the blood of
mammals

LOOKALIKES:
There are several
very similar
species with
different
abdomen and
wing markings

These distinctive little flies are often admired
at first for their attractive shape and colours –
until they pierce the skin, when a painful
wound ensues. They are closely related to the
other horseflies, though are noticeably
different in holding their wings at rest in a
triangle. The females fly very quietly and
settle inconspicuously. The larvae live in wet
soil and mud, and the adults are most likely to
be found in damp undisturbed sites such as
woods and wet heaths. They are widespread
through north and central Europe, and
uncommon in Britain.

TRUE FLIES, DIPTERA

J	F	M	A	M	J
J	A	S	O	N	D

Bee-fly
Bombylius major

ID FACT FILE

SIZE:
Body length
10–12 mm
(excluding the
proboscis, which
adds about
another 6mm)

DESCRIPTION:
A plump furry
brown fly, with
two wings (bees
have four) heavily
marked with
darker colours.
The long probos-
cis is always
noticeable

FOOD:
Adults feed on
nectar

LOOKALIKES:
There are several
smaller species.
*Thyridanthrax
fenestratus*
(p.158) is similar
but darker, and
lacking the
proboscis

Although it could be mistaken for a small
bumble bee, this appealing little insect differs
from them in having a long, and quite obvious,
thin proboscis which is held out in front of the
fly, even when it is resting. The larvae of the
Bee-fly live parasitically in the nests of solitary
bees and wasps. Bee-flies are quite mobile, and
can be found in a variety of grassy, flowery
sunny places, darting from flower to flower to
feed. They are common and widespread
throughout Europe.

Thyridanthrax fenestratus

J F M A M J
J A S O N D

ID FACT FILE

SIZE:
Body length
8–10 mm

DESCRIPTION:
A dark slightly
furry bee-like
insect, which
holds its wings in
a triangle when
at rest. The
wings are heavily
suffused with
dark colour,
within which
there are little
clear windows

FOOD:
Adults feed on
nectar

LOOKALIKES:
Anthrax anthrax
is similar, slightly
larger, and the
smoky wings
have no clear
windows

Although neither well-known nor conspicuous, this little fly is quite recognisable once seen. It resembles the bee-fly (p.157) in habitats, but is less furry, darker, and without a long proboscis. It moves quickly from flower to flower, like a bee-fly, though with a tendency to bask more. The larvae are parasitic on various caterpillars. It occurs in dry, sunny flowery habitats, often heathland and other acid areas. It is uncommon in Britain, but widespread and moderately frequent in north and central Europe.

| J | F | M | A | M | J |
| J | A | S | O | N | D |

A Robber Fly
Asilus crabroniformis

ID FACT FILE

SIZE:
Body length
22–30 mm

DESCRIPTION:
A predominantly
yellowish-brown
insect in general
appearance, with
orange-brown
bristles, brown-
tinted wings and
a yellow and
brown abdomen

FOOD:
Other insects,
caught in flight

LOOKALIKES:
Laphria flava
(p.160) is more
robust and
darker brown

This is one of the largest of the robber flies –
a small group of bristly predatory flies which
mainly catch other insects in mid-air. All the
robber flies have a powerful beak, with which
they quickly penetrate their victims, and very
hairy faces. In this species, the larvae feed in
mammal dung, often of grazing domestic
animals, so they are most frequent in pasture,
especially if there are plenty of flowers for
perches and to attract other insects. It is rare
and mainly southern in Britain, but more
widespread in Europe.

TRUE FLIES, DIPTERA

J	F	M	A	M	J
J	A	S	O	N	D

A Robber Fly
Laphria flava

ID FACT FILE

SIZE:
Body length
25 mm

DESCRIPTION:
A noticeably
robust and bristly
fly, with a
yellowish-brown
abdomen and
dark hairy thorax.
Like other robber
flies, it has
powerful
mouthparts and
a bristly face

FOOD:
Other insects

LOOKALIKES:
Other Laphria
species are
similar, such as
the smaller and
less hairy *L.
gilva*, which is
local in
deciduous woods

This species, and a few close relatives, are the
largest and most robust of the robber flies in
Europe. They spend much of their time
resting on logs in sunny clearings in
woodland, especially coniferous woodland,
from where they make brief darting forays
to catch passing flying insects. The larvae feed
in old pine logs and stumps. It is extremely
rare in Britain, and confined to the old
Caledonian pine forest in Scotland; it is more
widespread in central and northern Europe,
though never abundant.

TRUE FLIES, DIPTERA

J	F	M	A	M	J
J	A	S	O	N	D

Empid Fly
Empis tessellata

ID FACT FILE

SIZE:
Body length
10–12 mm

DESCRIPTION:
A dark-bodied
rather hairy fly.
The abdomen is
longitudinally
striped, and the
wings are
suffused with
brown. It has
long dark legs

FOOD:
Other insects,
and nectar

LOOKALIKES:
Hilara maura is
similar but
smaller, and the
males have
enlarged front
tarsi, on their
legs, used to
produce silk

The empid flies are closely related to the
robber flies, and have similar habits, but are
more slender, with less bristly faces, and a
long, slender downward-pointing proboscis.
They spend much of their time on and around
flowers such as hawthorn or angelica, where
they catch flies but also feed on nectar. This is
the most conspicuous member of the family. It
occurs in a variety of sheltered flowery
habitats, where insects are abundant, such as
woodland margins and rides, or scrub. It is
common and widespread throughout.

the enlarged front legs
of *Hilara maura* ×4

TRUE FLIES, DIPTERA

| J | F | M | A | M | J |
| J | A | S | O | N | D |

Poecilobothrus nobilitatus

ID FACT FILE

SIZE:
Body length
about 6 mm

DESCRIPTION:
The body is
metallic
greenish, with a
reddish tinge.
The wings are
marked with
smoky patches
in both sexes,
but white-tipped
only in males

FOOD:
Small
invertebrates

LOOKALIKES:
*Dolichopus
popularis* is
similar, but lacks
the patterned
wings, and males
do not have
white-tipped
wings

Despite its small size, this is quite a
conspicuous and attractive little fly. It occurs in
large numbers around water bodies where
there is some exposed mud and ample
emergent and floating vegetation. The males,
which have white-tipped wings, spend much of
their time either fighting each other, or
courting females by means of semaphor-like
wing movements. It is common and
widespread in much of Europe, but in Britain
it is common only in the southern part.

| J | F | M | A | M | J |
| J | A | S | O | N | D |

A Hoverfly
Episyrphus balteatus

ID FACT FILE

SIZE:
Body length
10–12 mm

DESCRIPTION:
The thorax is
dark brown, and
the narrow
abdomen is
marked with dou-
ble black stripes
on yellow, with
the upper stripe
bolder than the
lower

FOOD:
Nectar as adult,
aphids as larvae

LOOKALIKES:
Nothing looks
quite like it

This is probably the commonest and best-
known of the hoverflies, partly because it is a
frequent visitor to parks and gardens as well as
more natural habitats, but also because it can
occur in enormous numbers. The adults are
very mobile and migratory, and can appear in
vast swarms in some years, especially if the
winds are from the south. The larvae are
voracious aphid-feeders, and the adults may be
found almost anywhere that there are flowers
for nectar. It occurs throughout Europe.

HOVERFLIES, SYRPHIDAE

| J | F | M | A | M | J |
| J | A | S | O | N | D |

Syrphus ribesii

ID FACT FILE

SIZE:
Body length
10–12 mm

DESCRIPTION:
The thorax is
dark brown
edged with
yellowish hairs,
while the broad,
rounded
abdomen is
boldly marked
with yellow
stripes on black;
the uppermost
stripe is
interrupted

FOOD:
Nectar

LOOKALIKES:
Another hoverfly
*Megasyrphus
annulipes* has
very similar
markings, but is
much larger, and
less common

This is one of the commonest and best known
of the hoverflies, particularly because it is a
frequent visitor to parks and gardens as well as
more natural habitats. The adults are mobile
and active, and can turn up almost anywhere
that there are flowers to take nectar from. The
larvae are voracious aphid-feeders, and are
therefore welcome visitors to gardens; the
technique of companion planting,
interspersing vegetables with flowers, is
successful partly because it increases hoverfly
numbers, which come for the nectar.

aphid-eating hoverfly larva

HOVERFLIES, SYRPHIDAE

J	F	M	A	M	J
J	A	S	O	N	D

A Hoverfly
Scaeva pyrastri

ID FACT FILE

SIZE:
Body length
15 mm

DESCRIPTION:
The thorax is
dark black-brown
with paler hairs;
the abdomen is
similar, but with
three pairs of
large cream-
coloured comma-
shaped markings
down the sides

FOOD:
Nectar, as adult

LOOKALIKES:
S. selenitica has
the commas
markedly
thickened
towards the
centre of the
abdomen; it is
widespread
but local

This is one of the most distinctive of all
hoverflies with its particularly attractive
combination of colours and patterns. It is a
common species in parks, gardens, woodland
rides and almost anywhere that there are
flowers. Adults are very mobile – and numbers
may be boosted by large quantities of
immigrants in some years – so they can turn up
almost anywhere. The larvae are aphid-
feeders, like those of *Syrphus ribesii* (p.164)
and just as welcome to gardeners. It is
widespread throughout most of Europe.

the abdomens of *S. pyrastri* (right) and *S. selenitica*

HOVERFLIES, SYRPHIDAE

J	F	M	A	M	J
J	A	S	O	N	D

A Hoverfly
Rhingia campestris

ID FACT FILE

SIZE:
Body length
about 12–13 mm
including beak

DESCRIPTION:
The reddish-
brown beak is
the most
distinctive
feature. The
abdomen is
orange-brown,
with a central
black stripe,
though this is
variable

FOOD:
Nectar, as adult

LOOKALIKES:
A closely-related
species *R.
rostrata* has no
stripe on the
abdomen, and a
slightly shorter
beak. It is rarer

Although this is a rather undistinguished insect at first sight, it is actually quite distinctive once learnt by virtue of its curious robust almost triangular 'beak' or snout extending forwards from its face. The larvae feed in cow, and perhaps other mammalian, dung, and so it is most common in and around grazed pastures, particularly where there are flowers. Woodland rides and edges adjacent to pastures are the favoured sites. It is widespread and common throughout Britain and most of Europe.

| J | F | M | A | M | J |
| J | A | S | O | N | D |

A Hoverfly
Volucella pellucens

ID FACT FILE

SIZE:
Body length
15 mm

DESCRIPTION:
A large rather
shiny fly, which
settles with its
wings held in a
triangle. The
thorax is black,
then the
abdomen is half
white and half
black. The wings
are clear apart
from a smoky
patch on each

FOOD:
Nectar, as adult

LOOKALIKES:
*Leucozona
lucorum* is very
similar in
markings – *see*
under that
species for
differences

A large and strong-flying hoverfly, with
something of the character of a bumble-bee
about it, except that it is prone to hovering
frequently at about head-height, and it is
much shinier. It is a frequent visitor to
flowers, especially bramble and umbellifers
such as Angelica, for nectar. The eggs
are laid in wasps' nests, and adults have
been seen entering the nests quite
unhindered. This hoverfly is common and
widespread in sheltered flowery places
through Britain and most of Europe,
though rarely abundant.

J	F	M	A	M	J
J	A	S	O	N	D

A Hoverfly
Volucella zonaria

ID FACT FILE

SIZE:
Body length
20 mm

DESCRIPTION:
A large, boldly
marked species,
with a brownish
thorax, and a
yellow-orange
and black
banded
abdomen. The
wings are clear
with a slight
brownish
suffusion

FOOD:
Nectar

LOOKALIKES:
V. inanis is
similar but
smaller, yellower,
and with a more
pronounced
vertical line on
the abdomen

This is one of the largest and most spectacular of hoverflies, often mistaken for a wasp or hornet, thanks to its large size and yellow and black colouring, though it only has two wings and is a different shape to a wasp. It breeds in wasps' nests, like others in this group, though its full life-cycle is not known. It occurs in a variety of sheltered flowery habitats, including gardens, and is frequently seen visiting flowers such as bramble or sunbathing on fence posts. It is widespread in Europe, but local and southern in Britain, despite a recent expansion of range.

| J | F | M | A | M | J |
| J | A | S | O | N | D |

A Hoverfly
Volucella bombylans

ID FACT FILE

SIZE:
Body length
12–15 mm

DESCRIPTION:
Variable, but
generally dark
brown with a buff
or white 'tail' to
the abdomen;
always very hairy.
The wings are
clear except for a
patch of brown in
the centre of the
front margin

FOOD:
Nectar

LOOKALIKES:
It most
resembles
bumble bees,
superficially (*see*
above for
differences)

A robust and unusual Hoverfly that clearly
mimics bumble-bees. It is much hairier than
other hoverflies, like bumble bees, and it
occurs in different colours and patterns to
closely resemble different species of bumble
bee. It can be distinguished from them by
having only 2 wings, and by its lazier habits and
hovering flight. The eggs are laid in wasps'
nests, like other species in this genus. It is
common and widespread in flowery parts of
woodland, such as glades and rides, and occurs
virtually throughout Europe.

a white-tailed form
of *V. bombylans*

HOVERFLIES, SYRPHIDAE

J	F	M	A	M	J
J	A	S	O	N	D

A Hoverfly

Helophilus pendulus

ID FACT FILE

SIZE:
Body length
9–11 mm

DESCRIPTION:
The thorax is
clearly marked
with longitudinal
yellow stripes on
brown, which
quickly mark out
this genus. The
abdomen is
marked with
black on yellow

FOOD:
Nectar

LOOKALIKES:
There are several
similar species
in the same
genus; *H.
hybridus* differs
only in having
less yellow on
the legs, and
slightly different
markings (*see*
illustration)

This pretty little hoverfly is occasionally known
as the 'Sun-fly' for its habit of basking on leaves
and other surfaces in the sun. The larvae are
found in mud, manure, rotting sawdust and
other places rich in organic material. Adults
are common near such places, but they wander
widely and can turn up almost anywhere that
there are flowers to feed on. Its preferred
habitats are sheltered flowery places such as
woodland glades and gardens, and it is
common throughout Europe.

the closely related
H. hybridus

HOVERFLIES, SYRPHIDAE

J	F	M	A	M	J
J	A	S	O	N	D

Conops quadrifasciata

ID FACT FILE

SIZE:
Body length
11–13 mm
including
proboscis

DESCRIPTION:
There is a long
dark brown
proboscis. The
thorax is dark
brown, and the
abdomen is
banded yellow
and black, rather
like a wasp.
There is even a
distinct 'waist',
like in
hymenoptera

FOOD:
Nectar as adult

LOOKALIKES:
There are several
similar species,
needing detailed
examination to
separate them

The conopid flies differ from hoverflies in
having a more hunched and 'waisted'
appearance, and they do not normally hover.
The larvae of most are internal parasites of
bumble bees, feeding within the bee. The adults
are rather slow-moving insects, lazily visiting
flowers such as Angelica or ragwort. They occur
in a wide variety of dry sunny flowery situations,
such as chalk grassland, though they are rarely
common. They are widespread but local both in
Britain and most of Europe.

J	F	M	A	M	J
J	A	S	O	N	D

Thistle Gall-fly
Urophora cardui

ID FACT FILE

SIZE:
Body length
6–7 mm

DESCRIPTION:
The adult flies
have a dark
tapering conical
body. The wings
are more
distinctive, with a
zig-zag dark
brown pattern.
The galls are
green or
brownish-green,
ovoid, on the
stems of thistle

FOOD:
Plant material

LOOKALIKES:
There are many
other 'picture-
wing' flies, some
of which cause
galls or mines,
such as the
Celery Fly *Euleia
heraclei*

The actual gall-fly is rarely noticed, though it is
quite distinctive; however, the effects that its
larvae cause are much more conspicuous. The
female lays eggs into the stems of thistles,
mainly creeping thistles, which develop into
large green ovoid galls with several chambers,
each with a larva. The adults spend much time
on the leaves of the thistle, using their picture-
wings to communicate with each other. It is
common and widespread wherever creeping
thistle occurs, throughout Europe.

gall on Creeping Thistle, life size

adult Thistle Gall-fly ×3

J	F	M	A	M	J
J	A	S	O	N	D

A Tachinid Fly

Tachina fera

ID FACT FILE

SIZE:
Body length
10–14 mm

DESCRIPTION:
A squat orange-brown fly, with a broad dark line down its abdomen, yellowish bases to the wings, and long bristles on the body

FOOD:
Nectar as an adult

LOOKALIKES:
T. grossa is darker and about twice the size. It is less common

The tachinid flies are a group of bristly parasitic flies, mostly attacking the larvae of other insects such as moths. This species attacks moth caterpillars of various species, killing them before it emerges. As an adult, it is frequent in damp woodlands and flowery marshy places, where they spend much time feeding on Angelica and other flowers, or basking in the sun. It is widespread almost throughout Britain and Europe, though rarely abundant, like most parasitic species.

J	F	M	A	M	J
J	A	S	O	N	D

Holly Leaf Gall
Phytomyza ilicis

ID FACT FILE

SIZE:
Body length
2–3 mm

DESCRIPTION:
The adult fly is
small, black and
undistinguished,
with clear wings.
The mines are
yellowish-brown
blotches covering
up to about a
third of the leaf
surface

FOOD:
The larvae feed
on the holly leaf

LOOKALIKES:
There are many
flies similar to
the adults, but
none cause
similar galls
on holly

This is one of a group of gall or mine-causing
flies. The adults are small and inconspicuous,
hard to identify without detailed
magnification; however, the galls are a
frequent and conspicuous sight on holly
leaves at almost all times of year. The larvae
or pupae are only present in spring and early
summer, but the mine remains visible. The fly
seems to occur almost anywhere that there
are holly trees – in woods, parks, hedges and
gardens, even in quite urban areas. It is
widespread throughout Britain and Europe
wherever there is holly.

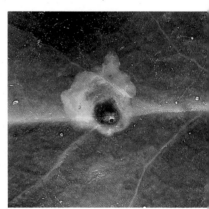

gall on holly leaf

adult Holly Leaf Gall fly ×5

J	F	M	A	M	J
J	A	S	O	N	D

Flesh-fly

Sarcophaga carnaria

ID FACT FILE

SIZE:
Body length
12–19 mm

DESCRIPTION:
They have red
eyes, a grey and
black striped
thorax, and a
chequered grey
and black
abdomen. The
large pad-like
feet are often
conspicuous

FOOD:
Nectar, or rotting
meat

LOOKALIKES:
There are several
similar species,
needing detailed
examination to
separate them

These are not the most popular of flies, due to
their strong association with rotting meat and
possible disease transmission, though they are
quite attractive with their chequered body and
red eyes. The adults often feed on nectar from
flowers, but they will also seek out rotting
flesh, where the females lay larvae rather than
eggs, to make rapid use of the food source.
They can occur almost anywhere, particularly
around farms and houses, and often bask in the
sunshine when not feeding.

J	F	M	A	M	J
J	A	S	O	N	D

Noon-fly

Mesembrina meridiana

ID FACT FILE

SIZE:
Body length
9–10 mm

DESCRIPTION:
The body is shiny black, and the wings have a large brownish-orange patch at the base, next to the body. They are held to form a triangle when at rest.

FOOD:
Nectar

LOOKALIKES:
Nothing similar in UK; *M. mystacea* is larger, with a brown thorax – it is widespread in north and central Europe

Although related to house-flies and sweat-flies, this species has little direct contact with man, and is quite harmless. The adults are fond of sunbathing on tree-trunks or walls, often in groups, though they also spend time at flowers feeding on nectar. The larvae feed in cattle and other mammalian dung, and the flies can be found almost anywhere suitable. They are especially common on the edges of woods with pasture nearby, and occur throughout Britain and Europe.

HOVERFLIES, SYRPHIDAE

J	F	M	A	M	J
J	A	S	O	N	D

Yellow Dung-fly
Scathophaga stercoraria

ID FACT FILE

SIZE:
Body length
9–11 mm

DESCRIPTION:
A rather narrow-bodied fly; males are yellowish with yellow hairs, while females are less hairy and greyish-green. The antennae are black in both sexes

FOOD:
Predatory on other flies

LOOKALIKES:
Other closely related species occur, with orange antennae

These are familiar, albeit not very popular flies. They swarm around cow dung in large numbers, and the golden-haired males are particularly conspicuous. They are very active flies, constantly mating, laying eggs, or making forays to catch other flies attracted to the dung. They are common and widespread in a variety of habitats, especially well-used pastures with woodland nearby. They occur throughout Britain and Europe in suitable habitats, and may often be abundant.

ANTS, BEES, WASPS AND SAWFLIES, HYMENOPTERA

J	F	M	A	M	J
J	A	S	O	N	D

Horntail

Urocerus gigas

ID FACT FILE

SIZE:
Body length up to
50 mm including
the ovipositor

DESCRIPTION:
Females are
banded black and
yellow, with a
long ovipositor.
Males are much
smaller, and the
abdomen is
tipped with a
short black spine.
There are two
large yellow spots
behind the eyes

FOOD:
Larvae feed in
coniferous wood;
adults feed little

LOOKALIKES:
One similar
species (not in
the UK) is *U.
augur*, which has
a yellow band
behind the eyes

This impressive insect is easily mistaken for a
hornet or wasp, though it is quite harmless.
The long ovipositor of the female – which gives
rise to the name Horntail – is used to lay eggs
into pine wood, but they do not sting. The
larvae develop in the wood for 2–3 years, and
may emerge long after the wood has been cut
and used. They are frequent, though never
common, in and around coniferous woods –
hence the alternative name of giant wood
wasp. They occur locally throughout Britain
and Europe.

J	F	M	A	M	J
J	A	S	O	N	D

Robin's Pincushion

Diplolepis rosae

ID FACT FILE

SIZE:
Body length
adults 4–5 mm;
galls up to
8–10 cm across

DESCRIPTION:
The gall wasps
have a blackish
thorax and a red
abdomen, with
rather smoky
wings. The galls
are spherical,
spiky, green at
first but
becoming red

FOOD:
Adults rarely feed

LOOKALIKES:
No galls look
similar

This is one of the most familiar and distinctive
of all galls, caused by a tiny black and red gall
wasp that most people never see. The galls are
multi-chambered inside, each containing a
developing larva. The females lay eggs without
fertilisation, and the males are very rare. The
galls can be found on rose-bushes of various
sorts, both wild and domesticated, and become
a distinctive feature in autumn as they redden,
and the rose leaves fall off. This species is
widespread and common throughout most of
Britain and Europe.

Robin's Pincushion on rose

adult gall-wasp ×3

currant gall Apr–Jun;
spangle gall Aug–Nov

ID FACT FILE

SIZE:
Body length:
adult insects are
2–3 mm long;
the spangle galls
are 4–6 mm
across, the
currant galls
slightly larger

DESCRIPTION:
The adults are
blackish and
inconspicuous.
The spangle galls
are circular,
highest in the
centre, yellowish
speckled with
red. The currant
galls are
spherical and red

FOOD:
The adults rarely
feed

LOOKALIKES:
The Smooth
Spangle Gall *N.
albipes* is found
on oak leaves
but is more
saucer-shaped
with curled-up
edges

Spangle Galls
Neuroterus quercusbaccarum

The Spangle Galls are familiar structures on
oak leaves in autumn, caused by gall wasps.
However, this species of gall wasp shows
alternation of generations, causing a quite
different gall for part of its life-cycle; in spring,
the females lay eggs into oak buds, causing
currant galls (looking just like redcurrants) on
the developing male oak catkins. They are
common and widespread wherever suitable oak
trees occur, including single trees in parks and
gardens, and are found throughout Europe.

Spangle Galls on oak leaf (with Silk Button Galls,
bottom left)

cross-sections of Spangle Gall
(left) and Smooth Spangle Gall

J	F	M	A	M	J
J	A	S	O	N	D

adults Jun–Jul;
galls May–Nov

Oak Apple
Biorrhiza pallida

Oak Apples are amongst the most familiar and distinctive of galls, and in some parts of Britain, an Oak Apple day is celebrated on May 29th in commemoration of the restoration of the monarchy. The large spongy globes contain numerous chambers with the larvae of a Gall-wasp in them, and these are themselves often parasitised by other insects. Oak Apples are widespread and common on oaks, especially common oak, including young trees, wherever they occur, though it is much less common in urban areas. It occurs throughout Britain and Europe in lowland areas.

ID FACT FILE

SIZE:
Body length: adults 3–4 mm; the 'apples' are up to 4–5 cm across

DESCRIPTION:
The adult gall-wasp is orange-brown. The galls are spongy irregular spheres, greenish at first but becoming browner, and disintegrating through the autumn

FOOD:
Adults rarely feed

LOOKALIKES:
Although not similar, the Marble Gall *Andricus kollari* is often mistaken for Oak Apple – it is smaller, harder and more regularly spherical. Common throughout

Oak Apple on oak

Marble Galls

ANTS, BEES, WASPS AND SAWFLIES, HYMENOPTERA

J	F	M	A	M	J
J	A	S	O	N	D

An Ichneumon Fly

Rhyssa persuasoria

ID FACT FILE

SIZE:
Body length
30 mm or more,
with the
ovipositor almost
as long again

DESCRIPTION:
The body is black
with white
markings, with a
long black
ovipositor at the
tip. The legs are
orange-red

FOOD:
Adults feed little,
though may visit
flowers at times

LOOKALIKES:
None

Ichneumons are a very large family of parasitic insects, which are generally very hard to identify with certainty. This species is one of the largest ichneumons, and distinctive in its markings and shape. It is parasitic on the Horntail (p.178), and the female ichneumon detects the Horntail larvae deep in the timber, then uses her very long drill-like ovipositor to place an egg next to it. It is widespread and moderately common in coniferous woodland where horntails occur, throughout most of Britain and Europe.

J	F	M	A	M	J
J	A	S	O	N	D

Yellow Ophion

Ophion luteus

ID FACT FILE

SIZE:
Body length
15–20 mm

DESCRIPTION:
The whole body
is reddish-orange
in colour, while
the head is
yellow with black
eyes. The wings
are clear except
for an orange
front margin

FOOD:
Rarely feeds as
adult

LOOKALIKES:
*Netelia
testaceus* is
similar, but has
a dark-tipped
abdomen; there
are other similar
Ophion species,
too

This is one of the few ichneumons that is
noticed by non-entomologists, thanks to its
habit of coming into houses at night
sometimes. It is parasitic on the caterpillars of
various moths, in which the eggs are laid
directly. If caught, the female is prepared to
use her sharp ovipositor to defend herself. It
occurs frequently in a wide variety of more
natural habitats, such as woods, scrub and
older parks and gardens, though its nocturnal
habits make it easily overlooked. It is
widespread through most of Europe.

Apanteles glomeratus

ID FACT FILE

SIZE:
Body length
2–3 mm

DESCRIPTION:
The adult is a
small slender
black-bodied
insect, with clear
wings and
orange legs. The
pupae are yellow,
sausage-shaped
and furry

FOOD:
Larvae feed
inside the
butterfly
caterpillars

LOOKALIKES:
None

This little insect is one of the braconid wasps, closely related to the icheumons. The adults are small, black and easily missed, though they are often quite visible in cabbage patches in early summer, as they fly about seeking cabbage white butterfly caterpillars. They are most noticeable at the pupal stage; the larvae emerge from the nearly mature caterpillar and pupate around its shrunken skin in yellow furry cocoons. It is common and widespread throughout, wherever the host butterflies occur, and is especially noticeable in gardens.

Apanteles pupae around Cabbage White caterpillar

adult braconid wasp ×5

J	F	M	A	M	J
J	A	S	O	N	D

Ruby-tailed Wasp
Chrysis ignita

ID FACT FILE

SIZE:
Body length
8–12 mm

DESCRIPTION:
A striking insect,
with a metallic
greenish-blue
head and thorax,
and a metallic
red abdomen.
The wings are
smoky-brown

FOOD:
Larvae feed on
the larvae of
mason wasps

LOOKALIKES:
There are many
similar species,
needing detailed
examination to
identify; *C. fulgida*
has the first
segment of the
abdomen green

Despite its small size, this is a striking little insect
thanks to its metallic jewel-like colours. They
resemble a small brightly coloured bee, and live
as parasites of mason bees. They have very hard
cuticles which allows the female to enter bees'
nests without getting stung, where they lay their
eggs; the developing larvae eat the larvae of the
host bee. They are most frequently seen
searching walls and sandy banks, where mason
bees occur, or sunning themselves nearby. It is
widespread and moderately common throughout
most of Britain and Europe.

J	F	M	A	M	J
J	A	S	O	N	D

Velvet Ant
Mutilla europaea

ID FACT FILE

SIZE:
Body length
13–15 mm

DESCRIPTION:
Females are
squat wingless
insects, with a
black head, a red
completely
unsegmented
thorax, and a
black abdomen
with patches of
yellowish hairs.
Males similar,
but winged and
with thorax
segments

FOOD:
The larvae of
bumble bees

LOOKALIKES:
Distinctive in the
UK; there are
similar species
in mainland
Europe, such as
the smaller
Myrmilla capitata

The Velvet Ant is a curious little insect that is
neither wasp nor ant, though the females are
wingless and somewhat resemble an ant. They
are parasitic on bumble bees, feeding on the
larvae within the nest. The males are fully
winged and mobile, and can occasionally be
seen sunning themselves on banks or stones. It
is a species of heathland and other dry open
areas where bumble bees occur. It is
widespread in both Britain and Europe, but
never common, and easily overlooked.

J	F	M	A	M	J
J	A	S	O	N	D

Wood Ant
Formica rufa

ID FACT FILE

SIZE:
Body length
10–12 mm

DESCRIPTION:
All stages are
largely black,
though the
workers (the
most commonly
seen stage) have
a red thorax and
red legs. The
nests are huge
conical piles of
plant material
such as pine
needles

FOOD:
Omnivorous, with
a preference for
invertebrate food

LOOKALIKES:
There are several
rather similar
wood ants

Wood Ants are amongst the most familiar and
distinctive of ants, partly because they are large
and occur in considerable abundance, but also
because they build huge nests. They live in
large colonies, and build nests of vegetation
which may reach 2m in height. From these,
the workers fan out in vast numbers, often on
clearly defined paths, to seek food and nesting
material. They are protected in some countries
because of their value in reducing forest pests.
They are widespread and common in north-
central Europe and mountain areas further
south, usually in coniferous woods.

J	F	M	A	M	J
J	A	S	O	N	D

Bee-killer Wasp

Philanthus triangulum

ID FACT FILE

SIZE:
Body length
Females are
largest, up to
18 mm; males
up to 10 mm

DESCRIPTION:
The head and
thorax are black,
while most of the
abdomen is pale
orange, often
with a black
triangle on each
segment

FOOD:
Adults feed little;
larvae live on
honey bees

LOOKALIKES:
None with quite
the same
combination of
characters

As its name suggests, this is a wasp that catches
and kills bees. In fact, just the females catch
bees, usually while they are feeding at flowers,
and they paralyse them with their sting, then
carry them to the nest site in a burrow. The
paralysed bees form a living food source for the
wasp's developing larvae. The bee-killer occurs
mainly on sandy soil such as heathlands, where
it is easy to dig burrows. It is widespread and
moderately frequent in most of Europe, except
the far north, but rare and southern in Britain.

J	F	M	A	M	J
J	A	S	O	N	D

Sand Wasp
Ammophila sabulosa

ID FACT FILE

SIZE:
Body length
18–25 mm

DESCRIPTION:
The head, thorax
and legs are
blackish; the
abdomen starts
black and very
narrow but
broadens and
becomes red,
tipped with
bluish-black

FOOD:
Females feed
little, males may
visit flowers for
nectar

LOOKALIKES:
There are several
similar species.
Podalonia hirsuta
is similar in
colour but has a
clearly defined
'stalk' which
expands rapidly
to the rest of the
abdomen

Sand Wasps are most often seen either running
busily over bare sandy soil, or dragging
caterpillars. The females seek out caterpillars of
various species – as long as they are plump and
not hairy – which they drag to their nest-burrow
and paralyse with a sting to provide food for the
developing larva. Each burrow normally
contains one caterpillar with one egg laid on it.
They are locally frequent in sandy places such as
heathland and sand dunes, throughout most of
Europe but mainly southern in Britain.

a closely related species *Podalonia hirsuta*

| J | F | M | A | M | J |
| J | A | S | O | N | D |

German Wasp
Vespula germanica

ID FACT FILE

SIZE:
Body length:
12–20 mm,
including the
larger queens

DESCRIPTION:
Familiar black
and yellow
banded insects,
with a blackish
thorax. The
markings on the
thorax and
abdomen are
important in
distinguishing
different species

FOOD:
Initially insects,
gradually
changing over to
fruit and nectar

LOOKALIKES:
Several similar
species;
common wasp *V.
vulgaris* differs in
small details,
e.g. in having an
anchor of black
on its face, not
three black dots.
Similar
distribution

This is one of the familiar wasps that come to seek out sweet substances in late summer, often coming into conflict with people in the process. In fact, there are several similar species known collectively as 'wasps' by the general public (*see* Fact File). They are social insects, living in colonies of hundreds or thousands of individuals, and it is the workers from the colonies that are most often seen. The nest itself is a delicate structure made from paper (chewed up wood), roughly spherical in shape. They are common and widespread in a variety of habitats, including gardens, throughout.

faces of Common Wasp (left) and German Wasp

J	F	M	A	M	J
J	A	S	O	N	D

Dolichovespula media

ID FACT FILE

SIZE:
Body length
15–30 mm,
larger than
common wasps

DESCRIPTION:
They are
distinctly larger
and darker than
the common
wasps, with
much larger
areas of black on
the abdomen.
The thorax has
slender yellow
stripes, and four
yellow spots

FOOD:
Similar to
common wasps

LOOKALIKES:
Other social
wasps are
generally quite
similar

This large, dark wasp is sometimes popularly
known as the 'killer wasp', though it is hardly a
fair description. It has a similar life-cycle to
other social wasps, living in small to medium-
sized colonies, in roughly globular nests hung
in trees and bushes. In Britain, it was rare and
local until recently, but has been spreading
quickly northwards in recent years; it is
widespread through most of Europe except the
far north. Preferred habitats include scrub,
open woodland and large gardens, wherever
there are suitable nest sites.

nest of *D. media*,
approximately ½th life-size

J	F	M	A	M	J
J	A	S	O	N	D

Hornet
Vespa crabro

ID FACT FILE

SIZE:
Body length
25–40 mm

DESCRIPTION:
The head and
face are orange,
the thorax and
first part of the
abdomen
reddish, and the
rest of the
abdomen yellow
with dark
markings

FOOD:
Insects, nectar
and other sugary
substances

LOOKALIKES:
In most of
Europe it is
unique; in south-
east Europe, the
Oriental Hornet
V. orientalis has
a brighter yellow
abdomen tipped
with brown

The hornet is the largest of the social wasps
over most of Europe, and is easily
distinguished by its size and reddish
colouring. Despite its size and fearsome
appearance and reputation, they are not
normally aggressive or harmful. The nest is
constructed in hollow trees or other cavities,
and the larvae are fed mainly on insects which
are caught effortlessly. It occurs in a variety of
habitats, especially lightly wooded areas and
parks, where there are old trees. In Britain it
is local and southern, while on the continent
it is more widespread.

J	F	M	A	M	J
J	A	S	O	N	D

Leaf-cutter Bee

Megachile centuncularis

ID FACT FILE

SIZE:
Body length
10 mm

DESCRIPTION:
The adult bee is
dark brown
above, with
bright orange
hairs under the
female's
abdomen, for
gathering pollen.
The cut leaves
are distinctive,
with semi-circular
holes in the
margin

FOOD:
Pollen and nectar

LOOKALIKES:
There are several
similar species,
such as *M.
maritima*, of
which the male
has enlarged
front legs

Although this little bee itself is not very
familiar, its effects are often noticed. The
females cut almost exactly semi-circular discs
of leaf material from the leaves of roses and
other plants, which they carry off to their nests
and use to make little cells for the developing
larvae. The nest is usually in a cavity in rotten
wood. They are widespread and common
through most of Britain and Europe except the
far north, in scrub, gardens, parks and the
open parts of woodland.

female Leaf-cutter Bee with leaf disc

rose leaf cut by
Leaf-cutter Bee

ANTS, BEES, WASPS AND SAWFLIES, HYMENOPTERA

| J | F | M | A | M | J |
| J | A | S | O | N | D |

Violet Carpenter Bee

Xylocopa violacea

ID FACT FILE

Size:
Body length
20–30 mm

Description:
The body is dark
blue-black,
covered with
short hairs. The
wings are
brownish,
appearing violet
from certain
angles

Food:
Nectar

Lookalikes:
In south Europe,
there are a few
similar species,
such as *X.
cyanescens*,
which is metallic
blue with dark
hairs

A large and impressive insect that is unlikely to be overlooked where it occurs. They fly noisily from flower to flower, taking nectar, though despite their size, they are harmless and unaggressive. They excavate nests in old timber, which accounts for the common name. In Britain, they are just an occasional vagrant, but they are widespread and quite common in south and central Europe. They can occur in any flowery places, especially if close to old woodland, and are very mobile.

J	F	M	A	M	J
J	A	S	O	N	D

Honey Bee
Apis mellifera

ID FACT FILE

SIZE:
Body length
10–15 mm

DESCRIPTION:
A rather plain
insect, mid-
brown and hairy,
with clear wings.
There are several
strains, such as
the Italian race
which has an
orange patch

FOOD:
Pollen and nectar

LOOKALIKES:
There are similar
solitary bees,
needing detailed
examination to
identify with
certainty

The Honey Bee is almost too well-known and
popular to need description. They are the
archetypal social insects, living in colonies of
up to 50,000 individuals. Although originally
from Asia, they are widespread throughout
most of Europe, and play a vital role in the
pollination of crops and wild flowers. Most of
the bees that we see are from hives, but wild
colonies do exist, and they are virtually all
worker bees (sterile females). They can occur
anywhere flowery, and hives are often moved
around to make particular use of a flower
display, such as heather.

| J | F | M | A | M | J |
| J | A | S | O | N | D |

queens overwinter

White-tailed Bumble Bee

Bombus lucorum

ID FACT FILE

SIZE:
Body length
Queens up to
20 mm, males
and workers
rather less

DESCRIPTION:
Mainly black and
furry, but with a
yellow collar on
the thorax, a
yellow band on
the abdomen,
and a white tail

FOOD:
Nectar and
pollen

LOOKALIKES:
Several species
look similar. *B.
hortorum* has
similar colours
but has the
yellow band
where thorax and
abdomen meet.
Common
throughout

Bumble bees are very familiar as a group, though few people realise how many different species there are in Europe, and they can be quite difficult to tell apart. The White-tailed Bumble Bee is one of the more distinctive (*see* Fact File). Like other bumble bees, they form annual colonies, usually in underground nests which will eventually contain queens, workers and males. It is a common species in almost all habitats, especially scrub, wood margins, rough grassland and gardens, throughout Britain and Europe.

the closely related
B. hortorum

J	F	M	A	M	J
J	A	S	O	N	D

ID FACT FILE

SIZE:
Body length
10–15 mm

DESCRIPTION:
Bright metallic
green insects,
with a variable
number of small
yellow spots and
stripes on the
elytra. The jaws
are large,
powerful and
white

FOOD:
Ground-dwelling
insects such as
ants

LOOKALIKES:
Wood Tiger
Beetle *C.
sylvatica* is
greyish-black,
with longer
yellow markings,
in woods and
heaths

Green Tiger Beetle
Cicindela campestris

The tiger beetles are active ground-dwelling
predators, normally visible during the daytime. If
disturbed, they fly for a short distance before
settling on the ground again. The larvae live in
vertical burrows in the ground, holding
themselves at the top in readiness for any prey;
once something is caught, they take it to the base
of the chamber to eat it. Green Tiger Beetles are
common in open sunny habitats, from lowland
heaths to mountain tundra, occurring virtually
throughout Britain and Europe.

larva of Tiger Beetle in its
chamber in the ground

BEETLES, COLEOPTERA

Violet Ground Beetle

Carabus violaceus

ID FACT FILE

SIZE:
Body length
25–35 mm

DESCRIPTION:
Predominantly
bluish-black in
colour with violet
edging around
the elytra. The
wing cases are
smooth

FOOD:
Various
invertebrates,
and some carrion

LOOKALIKES:
There are several
similar species;
C. nemoralis is
more greenish,
and the elytra
are pitted with
lines of holes

The ground beetles are active ground-dwelling predators, which feed mainly at night and hide under stones or logs during the day. This species catches and eats worms, slugs and other invertebrates, or it may feed on carrion at times. The larvae are more active than most larvae, and are predatory like the adults. They are common in a variety of habitats including woods, parkland and gardens, occurring virtually throughout Britain and Europe.

BEETLES, COLEOPTERA

Burying Beetle
Nicrophorus investigator

ID FACT FILE

SIZE:
Body length
15–25 mm

DESCRIPTION:
The head and
thorax are black,
and the wing-
cases have two
bright, jagged-
edged,
uninterrupted
bands across
them. The
antennae are
clubbed, with
orange tips

FOOD:
Carrion and
small insects

LOOKALIKES:
There are several
similar species;
N. interruptus is
closest, but with
the red bands
interrupted by
black in the
centre

The burying beetles are a small group of
mainly brightly coloured species. They gather
around a corpse and dig a hole beneath it,
eventually burying it, when the female lays her
eggs nearby. They feed on the corpse at the
same time, and on smaller insects that are
attracted to it. They are active fliers, able to
detect carrion at a considerable distance. This
species is widespread and moderately frequent
throughout, though never abundant. It can
occur in almost any habitat, wherever there are
corpses in suitable situations.

BEETLES, COLEOPTERA

Devil's Coach Horse
Staphylinus olens

ID FACT FILE

SIZE:
Body length
20–30 mm

DESCRIPTION:
The whole body
is black and
finely hairy,
narrowly
cylindrical and
flattened in
shape. The jaws
are powerful, and
the wing cases
are very short

FOOD:
Various insects
and other
invertebrates

LOOKALIKES:
*Creophilus
maximus* is
smaller, with
grey hairs; it is
particularly
associated with
dung

The Devil's Coach Horse is a member of the
very large family of rove beetles, with over 1000
species in Europe. Most of them are hard to
identify, but the Devil's Coach Horse is quite
distinctive by its size, shape and habitats. They
are mainly nocturnal, hiding under stones and
logs in the day, though they may venture out on
fine days to feed. When disturbed, it raises its
hind end and opens its jaws in a threat display,
and it can give a nasty bite. It is common and
widespread in scrub, parks, heaths and other
habitats, through most of Europe.

BEETLES, COLEOPTERA

J	F	M	A	M	J
J	A	S	O	N	D

Stag Beetle
Lucanus cervus

ID FACT FILE

SIZE:
Body length
up to 50 mm
(male), to 35 mm
(female)

DESCRIPTION:
The male antlers
are reddish,
while the head
and thorax of
both sexes are
black. The elytra
are usually dark
reddish-brown,
occasionally
black. Females
are smaller and
have no antlers

FOOD:
Adults feed on
sap, larvae on
decaying wood

LOOKALIKES:
None

This is one of the largest and most impressive
of European beetles, of which the males
cannot be confused with anything else. The
male beetle bears enlarged antler-shaped jaws,
with which it may engage other males in fights
during the breeding period. The larvae live in
dead wood, especially stumps, where they may
take several years to develop. It occurs in old
woods, parkland and even urban areas if there
are enough old trees. It is local and mainly
southern in Britain, but more widespread on
the continent.

Male Stag Beetle

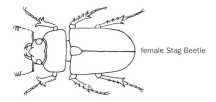

female Stag Beetle

BEETLES, COLEOPTERA

| J | F | M | A | M | J |
| J | A | S | O | N | D |

Dor Beetle
Geotrupes stercorarius

ID FACT FILE

SIZE:
Body length
20–25 mm

DESCRIPTION:
A wholly black
insect above.
The thorax is
smooth, and the
elytra have seven
distinct ridges on
each side.
Underneath, it is
metallic bluish or
green

FOOD:
Dung

LOOKALIKES:
G. spiniger is
very similar,
differing in minor
features such as
the less heavily
dotted elytra
stripes

The Dor Beetle is one of the commonest and
most conspicuous of the group known as the
dung beetles. They are attracted to dung,
especially cow-dung, where they dig burrows
below it which they provision with dung for the
developing larvae. They can fly well, most
frequently on warm evenings, and the name
'dor' comes from an old word meaning drone.
Its favoured habitat is pastures where suitable
dung can be found, and it occurs throughout
most of Britain and Europe, though confined
to mountains in southern Europe.

BEETLES, COLEOPTERA

Minotaur Beetle

Typhaeus typhoeus

ID FACT FILE

SIZE:
Body length
14–20 mm

DESCRIPTION:
A shiny black
beetle, with three
frontal
projections on
the male, as
described (the
female has two
short points),
and heavily
ribbed wing-
cases

FOOD:
Rabbit and
sheep dung

LOOKALIKES:
There are similar
species in the
extreme south of
Europe, but not
elsewhere

This is a very attractive and distinctive dung
beetle. The males have three forward-pointing
horns on the pronotum, with the shortest one
in the middle. They make deep cylindrical
burrows in sandy soil – often readily visible,
especially in spring – which they provision with
rabbit or sheep dung for the developing larvae.
The adults can fly well, and are most often
seen on warm evenings. They are common in
heathy places and dry pastures, throughout
most of Europe except the far north, though
mainly southern in Britain.

Minotaur Beetle rolling Rabbit dung

| J | F | M | A | M | J |
| J | A | S | O | N | D |

Cockchafer
Melolontha melolontha

ID FACT FILE

SIZE:
Body length
20–30 mm

DESCRIPTION:
They have a
black head and
thorax, and
brown sculptured
wing-cases, with
a very hairy body
below. The
antennae,
especially those
of the male, are
large and open
like a fan

FOOD:
Plant material

LOOKALIKES:
The Summer
Chafer
*Amphimallon
solstitialis* is
smaller with a
brown thorax and
pronotum, and
flies slightly later

The Cockchafer is one of the more familiar of the beetles, thanks to its habit of flying noisily about on warm early summer evenings and crashing into windows. It is also known as the May Bug, describing its normal season of appearance. The larvae live on the roots of grasses and other plants in permanent pasture, and were once so abundant as to be a pest. It is common and widespread in grassy and lightly wooded places throughout Britain and Europe except the far north.

J	F	M	A	J
J	A	S	O	N	D

Bee Beetle
Trichius fasciatus

ID FACT FILE

SIZE:
Body length
11–15 mm

DESCRIPTION:
A distinctive
beetle, with a
brownish-hairy
thorax, and
yellow or orange
elytra boldly
marked with 6
black curved
stripes, though
these are
variable in shape

FOOD:
Pollen

LOOKALIKES:
The most similar
is *T. rosaceus*,
which has a
more triangular
thorax;
widespread
except in the UK

Also known as the Bee Chafer, this beetle does slightly resemble a bee in its size and hairy thorax, though on closer examination the typical beetle wing-cases are visible. They are avid pollen feeders, normally seen visiting flowers such as bramble or wild rose buried amongst the anthers. The larvae live in dead wood, and their preferred habitat is where flowery pastures and old woodland occur together. It is widespread on mainland Europe, especially in hilly areas, though rare and local in Britain.

BEETLES, COLEOPTERA

J	F	M	A	M	J
J	A	S	O	N	D

Rose Chafer
Cetonia aurea

ID FACT FILE

SIZE:
Body length
15–21 mm

DESCRIPTION:
A bright green
metallic insect
above
(occasionally
dark green, or
bronze), usually
coppery red
below. The wing
cases are
marked with
small white
stripes

FOOD:
Pollen from
flowers including
roses

LOOKALIKES:
C. cuprea is very
similar, but the
elytra taper
towards the
back; in similar
habitats

An attractive and almost jewel-like beetle,
thanks to the bright metallic green thorax and
wing cases. They have a noisy bumbling flight,
suddenly settling on a flower to begin feeding
on the pollen. The larvae of this species live in
old timber, though closely-related species live
in ants' nests. They prefer flowery sheltered
places near or in older woodland, but the
adults are quite mobile and can turn up almost
anywhere, including in gardens. They are
common in southern and central Europe, but
less frequent in the UK.

the shapes of Rose Chafer
(left) and the related
Cetonia cuprea

BEETLES, COLEOPTERA

J	F	M	A	M	J
J	A	S	O	N	D

A Click Beetle
Athous haemorrhoidalis

ID FACT FILE

SIZE:
Body length
10–15 mm

DESCRIPTION:
A narrowly
cylindrical insect,
with a grey-brown
downy thorax,
and grooved,
shiny brown wing-
cases

FOOD:
Omnivorous

LOOKALIKES:
Ctenicera cuprea
is similar in
shape, but
darker and
shinier, with
feathery
antennae

The click beetles are a large family of beetles,
so-called because of their ability to suddenly
leap into the air with a loud click, usually after
they have been turned over, and land the right
way up. The larvae are soil-living, thin creatures,
known as wireworms, which may cause damage
to crops though they also eat invertebrates. It is
common and widespread in pastures, woodland
margins and rides and other rough habitats
throughout most of Britain and Europe.

*Ctenicera
cuprea*

BEETLES, COLEOPTERA

A Soldier Beetle
Cantharis rustica

ID FACT FILE

SIZE:
Body length
12–16 mm

DESCRIPTION:
They have red
and black heads,
a red thorax with
a black spot, and
dark bluish-black
soft elytra; the
legs are mainly
red

FOOD:
Small insects
and other
invertebrates

LOOKALIKES:
C. fusca is
similar with black
legs and a black
spot near the
front of the
thorax. Similar
habitats

The soldier beetles are a small group of
attractive beetles, so-called because of their
smart colours, reminiscent of an old-fashioned
soldier's uniform. They are active predators,
hunting on flowers and leaves in sunny
weather, looking for small insects. They can
also fly well at times, though tend not to. They
occur commonly in rough flowery places such
as woodland margins and glades, hedgerows
and scrub, and are widespread throughout most
of Britain and Europe, except the far north.

Cantharis fusca,
life-size

BEETLES, COLEOPTERA

| J | F | M | A | M | J |
| J | A | S | O | N | D |

Glow-worm

Lampyris noctiluca

ID FACT FILE

SIZE:
Body length
10–20 mm, with
the females
longer than
males

DESCRIPTION:
Males are dark
greyish-brown
with a yellowish
edge to the
pronotum;
females
resemble a
flattened three-
legged
woodlouse, with
orange edges to
the abdominal
segments

FOOD:
Larvae feed on
snails, adults
rarely feed

LOOKALIKES:
*Phausis
splendidula* is
smaller, and the
female is paler
with a different
light pattern.
Similar habitats,
not in UK

Despite their name, Glow-worms are a type
of beetle. The males are normal-looking
winged beetles which fly at night seeking out
the wingless females, which sit in grassy
places emitting a greenish glow from the tip
of the abdomen. They are predators on snails,
into which they inject digestive enzymes, so
they tend to occur in places where the right
species is abundant, such as chalk grassland,
flowery banks and woodland edges, but are
rare in places where there are a lot of lights.
They are widespread in Europe, mainly
southern in Britain.

female Glow-worm

adult male
Glow-worm ×1½

BEETLES, COLEOPTERA

Cardinal Beetle

Pyrochroa coccinea

ID FACT FILE

SIZE:
Body length
15–20 mm

DESCRIPTION:
The wing-cases
and thorax are
bright red. In this
species, the
small head is
black, as are the
legs and
attractive
feathery
antennae

FOOD:
Nectar, sap and
other sweet
liquids

LOOKALIKES:
A very similar
species with the
same English
name is *P.
serraticornis*
which has a red
head

The Cardinal Beetle is an attractive and
distinctive species, so-called because of its
bright red colouring. The larvae are predators
living under the bark of dead or dying trees
and stumps, so the adults tend to occur near
such features, especially where there are
abundant flowers. The adult beetles are rather
slow-moving, flying lazily from flower to
flower, or settling on tree-trunks. They are
widespread and moderately common through
north and central Europe (except the far
north), and throughout most of Britain.

BEETLES, COLEOPTERA

| J | F | M | A | M | J |
| J | A | S | O | N | D |

Eyed Ladybird
Anatis ocellata

ID FACT FILE

SIZE:
Body length
8–11 mm

DESCRIPTION:
It is generally a
pale orange-red,
with large black
yellow-edged
spots on the
elytra, and white
patches on the
black pronotum.
The shape is
typical of other
ladybirds

FOOD:
Aphids

LOOKALIKES:
None

The Eyed Ladybird is one of the largest of
ladybirds, so-called because each black spot
has a pale area around it, making them look
rather like eyes. Both adults and larvae feed on
aphids, mainly up in pine and spruce trees.
Their favoured habitat is coniferous woodland,
though they are quite mobile and occasionally
turn up elsewhere. Like some of the other
ladybirds, it overwinters as an adult, in a
dormant condition. It is moderately common
and widespread throughout most of Europe in
suitable habitats.

BEETLES, COLEOPTERA

Seven-spot Ladybird
Coccinella 7-punctata

ID FACT FILE

SIZE:
Body length
7–9 mm

DESCRIPTION:
Distinctive red
oval body, with
seven black dots
on the elytra. The
pronotum is
black with two
white dots.
Larvae are
greyish-blue with
yellow dots

FOOD:
Aphids

LOOKALIKES:
No other
common species
normally has
seven spots

This is the most familiar of ladybirds, and the one that is generally thought of as the typical ladybird. When handled, they exude a strong-smelling, acrid, yellowish fluid as a defence against predators, reinforced by their bright warning colours. Both adults and larvae are active aphid hunters, and are very welcome in gardens and amongst crops. The adults hibernate, often in clusters in a sheltered hollow. It is common and widespread throughout most of Britain and Europe, and migrates widely in high population years.

Ladybird larva

BEETLES, COLEOPTERA

Oedemera nobilis

ID FACT FILE

Size:
Body length
8–10 mm

Description:
Pale metallic
green and rather
slender. Males
have swollen
hind femora and
gapping elytra,
females have
neither of these
characters. The
antennae are
long

Food:
Pollen

Lookalikes:
O. virescens is
duller green

This is a common and widespread beetle,
which is easily recognised once learnt. The
males are particularly distinctive, with their
metallic green colouring, swollen hind legs,
and diverging wing cases that have a gap
between them. The adults are pollen feeders,
and regularly visit a wide variety of flowers
particularly yellow ones. The larvae develop
in the old stems of plants such as ragwort.
It is common and widespread in sunny,
flowery habitats throughout most of
Britain and Europe.

male

BEETLES, COLEOPTERA

J F M A M J
J A S O N D

Oil Beetle
Meloe proscarabeus

ID FACT FILE

SIZE:
Body length
Females up to
30 mm, males
smaller

DESCRIPTION:
Females are
large, all-black,
swollen insects,
with very short
wing cases
leaving most of
the abdomen
uncovered.
Males are
smaller and have
kinked antennae

FOOD:
Adults eat plants
such as
buttercups

LOOKALIKES:
M. violaceus is
more blue;
similar habitats
but less common

The Oil Beetle is a curious-looking beetle with an unusual life-history. The swollen females lay their eggs in crevices or holes, and the long-legged active larvae swarm out over nearby vegetation in hundreds. To survive, the larvae must attach themselves to a bee and get carried back to their nest, where they eat the larvae, and then turn into a more typical beetle larva themselves. From then on they eat honey. They occur in rough grassy flowery places such as chalk downland, and are widespread throughout Britain and Europe except the coldest parts.

BEETLES, COLEOPTERA

J	F	M	A	M	J
J	A	S	O	N	D

Musk Beetle
Aromia moschata

ID FACT FILE

Size:
Body length
20–35 mm

Description:
The head, thorax and wing-cases are all metallic green or bronze-green, variable in colour. The antennae are long and thick, particularly those of the male which may exceed the body length

Food:
Nectar

Lookalikes:
Spanish Fly (Blister Beetle) *Lytta vesicatoria* has much shorter antennae

The Musk Beetle is one of the longhorn beetles, so-called because of their long antennae; in this species, the male's antennae are longer than the female's. The larvae develop in old timber, especially that of willows and other deciduous trees. The adults are active in the day, and spend most of their time at flowers. Their preferred habitats are sunny glades in damp woodland, often in river valleys, though they can travel widely and may turn up in other habitats. They are local and mainly southern in Britain, but more widespread on the continent.

J	F	M	A	M	J
J	A	S	O	N	D

A Longhorn Beetle
Strangalia maculata

ID FACT FILE

SIZE:
Body length
15–20 mm

DESCRIPTION:
A brightly
coloured insect,
with black head
and thorax, and
yellow elytra
marked variably
with black,
especially
towards the tips.
The antennae
are about as
long as the body

FOOD:
Pollen

LOOKALIKES:
A close relative
S. quadrifasciata
has four definite
yellow stripes
across the elytra;
similar habitats,
less common

This is one of the most familiar and
conspicuous of the longhorn beetles. It is
active by day, visiting flowers such as those of
dogrose, from which it eats quantities of
pollen. Although they can fly, they are
reluctant to do so, and are usually quite easily
approached. The larvae live in rotting tree
trunks and stumps. They are most frequent in
flowery glades and rides in old woodland,
though can also turn up along hedgerows and
in flowery grassland. It is a common and
widespread species throughout most of Britain
and Europe except the coldest parts.

J	F	M	A	M	J
J	A	S	O	N	D

Wasp Beetle
Clytus arietis

ID FACT FILE

SIZE:
Body length
10–18 mm

DESCRIPTION:
A slender beetle,
basically black
but with variable
yellow bands
behind the head
and across the
wing-cases. The
antennae are
relatively short,
about half the
body length

FOOD:
Nectar and
pollen

LOOKALIKES:
*Plagionotus
arcuatus* is
larger, with
thinner yellow
stripes and two
yellow dots on
the pronotum. It
is less common

Although small, this is a distinctive and
attractive little longhorn beetle, which bears a
passing resemblance to common wasps thanks
to its black and yellow banding, though it is
quite harmless. The larvae live in dead and
decaying timber, and the adults are most
often seen visiting flowers to feed, or
wandering about on logs. The preferred
habitats are woodland margins and rides,
parkland and even old gardens. It is
widespread and moderately common in
Britain and most of Europe except the far
north and south.

BEETLES, COLEOPTERA

Asparagus Beetle
Crioceris asparagi

ID FACT FILE

SIZE:
Body length
5–8 mm

DESCRIPTION:
The head is
black, and the
thorax orange-
red. The wing
cases are shiny
black with six
squarish creamy
dots and a
reddish margin.
The larvae are
greyish with
black spots

FOOD:
Asparagus
shoots

LOOKALIKES:
None

Asparagus Beetles are attractive and
distinctive little insects, but are not generally
welcome thanks to the habit both adults and
larvae have of eating asparagus shoots. They
are often abundant on cultivated asparagus –
where they are considered a pest – but also
occur on wild asparagus in rough grassy
places, especially near the coast. The adults
feed openly during the day, and are probably
protected from predators by their bright
warning colours. It is widespread in
southern and central Europe, and the
southern half of Britain.

J	F	M	A	M	J
J	A	S	O	N	D

Bloody-nosed Beetle

Timarcha tenebricosa

ID FACT FILE

SIZE:
Body length
12–20 mm

DESCRIPTION:
A squat, domed
beetle, entirely
black with
smooth wing
cases. The feet
are large and
almost paddle-
like

FOOD:
Adults and larvae
feed on
bedstraws and
other plants

LOOKALIKES:
None

A curiously endearing little beetle. The adults are slow-moving and flightless, and can therefore be easily approached and picked up. Their name comes from the habit they have of exuding a pool of orange-red fluid from their mouth when alarmed, presumably to deter predators. The larvae have a similar hunched shape, and can be seen on the food-plant, bedstraws and relatives. The beetles are widespread and locally common in rough grassy places, especially near the coast, throughout the warmer parts of Britain and south/central Europe.

Bloody-nosed Beetle
larva on bedstraw

BEETLES, COLEOPTERA

J	F	M	A	M	J
J	A	S	O	N	D

Mint Beetle
Chrysolina menthastri

ID FACT FILE

SIZE:
Body length
10 mm

DESCRIPTION:
A rounded
almost
hemispherical
beetle, bright
metallic green all
over

FOOD:
Mint and related
plants

LOOKALIKES:
Any metallic
green beetle on
mint is almost
certain to be this
species

Mint Beetles are attractive and jewel-like
beetles, clearly visible on their host plants, the
mints. They are daytime feeders, chewing on
the leaves of mint, or occasionally dead-nettles,
usually in damp sheltered places. It may
become very abundant at times, especially on
garden mint patches. They are one of a group
of rounded plant-feeding beetles known as the
leaf beetles. It is common and widespread
through southern and central Europe,
including Britain.

BEETLES, COLEOPTERA

| J | F | M | A | M | J |
| J | A | S | O | N | D |

Poplar Leaf Beetle
Chrysomela populi

ID FACT FILE

SIZE:
Body length
9–11 mm

DESCRIPTION:
The head and
pronotum are
bronze-green or
blackish, and the
elytra are bright
shiny red, though
fading with age,
with a tiny black
spot at the tip.
The legs and
antennae are
black

FOOD:
Leaves of willows
and poplars

LOOKALIKES:
C. tremulae
occurs on the
closely related
aspen; it is
smaller and
lacks the black
spots

This bright red beetle stands out clearly as it
feeds openly on the leaves of poplars and
willows. It varies greatly in abundance from
year to year, with a year of abundance often
being followed by a poor year. The larvae,
which also feed on willows and poplars, give off
a strong tarry smell when touched, reducing
their attractiveness to predators. It occurs in a
variety of habitats, such as woodland, dunes
and tundra, wherever willows or poplars occur,
throughout Britain and Europe.

J	F	M	A	M	J
J	A	S	O	N	D

Colorado Beetle
Leptinotarsa decemlineata

ID FACT FILE

SIZE:
Body length
10 mm

DESCRIPTION:
A boldly marked
beetle with
orange head and
pronotum,
marked with
black, and yellow
elytra striped
longitudinally
with black

FOOD:
Potato and
nightshade
plants

LOOKALIKES:
None

A well-known and much-feared insect, with distinctive shape and markings. It came originally from North America, but is widely established through much of Europe, especially the south, as a pest of potatoes, though it will also feed on other members of the nightshade family such as bittersweet. The adults and larvae can quickly reduce healthy plants to a blackened mess, so its presence is taken very seriously. It occurs in a variety of open grassy places, and potato crop fields or gardens.

the eggs of Colorado Beetle
on a potato leaf

BEETLES, COLEOPTERA

J	F	M	A	M	J
J	A	S	O	N	D

Hazel Weevil

Apoderus coryli

ID FACT FILE

SIZE:
Body length
5–7 mm

DESCRIPTION:
An attractive
bright orange-red
weevil, with a
shiny black
triangular to bell-
shaped head,
narrowest at the
rear end.

FOOD:
Hazel leaves and
fruit

LOOKALIKES:
Red oak roller
Attabelus nitens
is very similar,
but with a
rectangular black
head; common
on oaks

The weevils are a large and distinctive group of
beetles, most of which have a long snout with
jaws at the tip and antennae halfway along. The
Hazel Weevil is not quite typical in this respect,
though it has a curiously-shaped head that
narrows backwards towards the pronotum. They
occur on hazel bushes and other deciduous
trees, and the larvae feed inside rolled-up
leaves. It occurs in woodlands and scrub,
wherever hazel occurs, and is widespread
throughout most of Britain and Europe.

BEETLES, COLEOPTERA

J F M A M J
J A S O N D

Great Diving Beetle
Dytiscus marginalis

ID FACT FILE

SIZE:
Body length
28–38 mm;
larvae up to
50 mm

DESCRIPTION:
They are
basically deep
greenish-black in
colour, with pale
orange margins
around the
pronotum and
wing cases.
Females are less
shiny than
males, and have
more deeply
furrowed elytra

FOOD:
Voracious
predators on
invertebrates,
tadpoles and
small fish

LOOKALIKES:
*Cybister
laterimarginalis*
is similar, but
has yellow only
on the sides of
the pronotum,
not all round.
Widespread, but
not in UK

This is a large and impressive water beetle. Both the adults and the fearsome larvae are voracious predators, and will attack almost anything edible including small fishes and tadpoles – they should never be placed in an aquarium, as they rapidly kill everything else off! They are quite frequent in well-vegetated still and slow-flowing waters, including ditches. The adults, unusually amongst insects, may live for up to three years. It is widespread throughout most of Europe except the driest parts of the south.

Great Diving Beetle larva

J F M A M J
J A S O N D

Whirligig Beetles
Gyrinus natator

ID FACT FILE

SIZE:
Body length
7–10 mm

DESCRIPTION:
Blackish oval
beetles, with
finely striated
elytra. The two
rear pairs of legs
are very short,
like little oars

FOOD:
Carrion and
surface-dwelling
insects

LOOKALIKES:
Hairy Whirligig
*Orectochilus
villosus* is
slightly larger,
hairier and
nocturnal.
Occurs
throughout
except the
far north

The whirligig beetles are very familiar as the
small black beetles that whirl around,
apparently aimlessly, on the surface of water in
groups. They have eyes with two parts, one for
seeing above water and one for seeing below
water level. They feed on carrion and insects at
the water surface, including mosquito larvae.
The eggs are laid on submerged plants, and the
larvae are aquatic. Whirligig beetles are most
frequent in well-vegetated still and slow-moving
water bodies, throughout Britain and Europe.

SPIDERS, ARANEAE

J	F	M	A	M	J
J	A	S	O	N	D

Dysdera crocata

ID FACT FILE

SIZE:
Body length
12–15 mm
(female), 10 mm
(male)

DESCRIPTION:
The jaws are
large and
thickened, the
same colour as
the red-brown
carapace. The
abdomen is
smooth and
greyish-brown

FOOD:
Woodlice

LOOKALIKES:
D. erythrina is
slightly smaller,
with fewer spines
on legs; it is less
common

Although it has no English name, this is a very
distinctive and easily recognised spider, though
its largely nocturnal habits mean that it is easily
overlooked. It is one of a small group of spiders
that have their jaws modified to catch woodlice
(p.245), which most spiders cannot do. They
live under logs and stones, usually in warm
humid places where woodlice are abundant,
and it is often common in gardens. It is
widespread and moderately common in
Britain, except the far north, and through
Europe excluding Scandinavia.

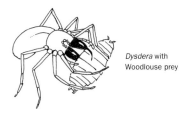

Dysdera with
Woodlouse prey

SPIDERS, ARANEAE

Daddy Long-legs Spider
Pholcus phalangioides

ID FACT FILE

SIZE:
Body length
8–10 mm

DESCRIPTION:
The most
distinctive
feature is the
very long slender
legs, and the
habit of resting
upside-down. The
carapace and
abdomen are
both pale
greyish-brown

FOOD:
Insects

LOOKALIKES:
P. opilionoides is
smaller, to
5 mm, with
minor anatomical
differences

This is one of the better-known spiders, thanks
to its distinctive appearance, curious habits,
and frequent choice of houses and sheds for its
home. They live upside-down on a rather
formless web, and if disturbed will shake and
whirl their bodies so fast that they become
blurred, as a defence against predators. The
eggs are carried by the female, and each of the
few large eggs is readily visible. It is common
in outhouses, cellars, caves and similar
habitats, throughout Britain and Europe,
except for the coldest areas.

SPIDERS, ARANEAE

May–Sept for females, spring only for males

ID FACT FILE

SIZE:
Body length
Female
12–15 mm, male
smaller

DESCRIPTION:
Both sexes have
green legs;
females
otherwise green
with a yellow
patch on the
abdomen; males
have a yellow
and red-striped
abdomen;
spiderlings are
red-dotted

FOOD:
Insects

LOOKALIKES:
None

female

male

Micrommata virescens

This is a beautiful and distinctive spider, with
the females a clear green all over, and the
males having a yellow abdomen with a red
stripe. They catch their prey without the use of
webs, mainly by waiting for it to come to them,
rather than pursuing it, and their green colour
probably helps to camouflage them. The
female makes a cell from silk and leaves, for
the egg sac. It occurs locally in damp heathy or
wooded sites, though never common. It is
widespread through most of Britain and
Europe, except the coldest parts.

J	F	M	A	M	J
J	A	S	O	N	D

A Crab Spider
Misumena vatia

ID FACT FILE

SIZE:
Body length
Female 10 mm,
male 4–5 mm

DESCRIPTION:
Crab-like in
shape, with a
round plump
body; the colour
may be white,
yellow or green,
with or without
red dots. Males
are much smaller
and brown

FOOD:
Various insects

LOOKALIKES:
Heriaeus hirtus
can be similar in
shape and colour
(green), but is
distinctly hairy.
Widespread in
central and
south Europe,
not in the UK

The crab spiders resemble crabs in their general shape, and they all have the habit of sitting motionless on a flower, which they may often resemble, simply waiting for insects to visit. Anything that comes within range, including large insects such as butterflies and bumble bees, is grasped and quickly paralysed. This species is able to change colour slowly to match its background, within the range of white, yellow and green. It is widespread and common throughout, except the far north, in warm flowery places.

female Crab Spider
with prey

SPIDERS, ARANEAE

Zebra Spider
Salticus scenicus

ID FACT FILE

SIZE:
Body length
6 mm

DESCRIPTION:
The carapace is
black with two
white dots, and
the abdomen is
black with white
stripes – hence
the name
'zebra'. The legs
are mainly black,
with white
patches

FOOD:
Insects

LOOKALIKES:
S. cingulatus is
similar but with
more white on
the abdomen
and legs; mainly
on trees

Although very small, this is quite a familiar
spider, well-enough known to have a common
name. It is one of the jumping spiders, and it
spends its time stalking prey then leaping on it,
and they can easily jump gaps that are in their
line of progress. It will tackle prey that is much
larger than itself, which it quickly paralyses.
They are most common on walls and rocks,
being active in sunny weather, but hidden in a
crevice when it's dull. It is widespread
throughout Britain and Europe, except the
coldest areas.

J	F	M	A	M	J
J	A	S	O	N	D

A Wolf Spider
Arctosa perita

ID FACT FILE

SIZE:
Body length
8–9 mm

DESCRIPTION:
The carapace is
light to dark
brown with paler
markings, while
the abdomen is
brown with grey,
pink and white
markings. The
legs are long and
conspicuously
banded

FOOD:
Insect prey

LOOKALIKES:
There are other
similar wolf
spiders, though
this is the most
conspicuous

This species is one of the most distinctive of
the group known as wolf spiders, so-called
because they roam about and pounce on prey,
making no use of a web at all. They make
burrows in sand or under stones, but are active
daytime predators and are frequently seen
running about on sandy patches. Their colour
varies considerably, tending to match that of
the habitat. Their preferred habitats include
sandy heaths, dunes, and other sandy places. It
is common and widespread throughout Britain
and much of Europe.

SPIDERS, ARANEAE

J	F	M	A	M	J
J	A	S	O	N	D

Nursery Web Spider
Pisaura mirabilis

ID FACT FILE

Size:
Body length
10–15 mm

Description:
A relatively large
finely downy
spider; the
carapace is
greyish-brown
with a
longitudinal pale
stripe down the
centre; the
abdomen has
pale and dark
brownish-grey
areas

Food:
Insects

Lookalikes:
The Raft Spider
(p.233) is rather
similar, and
carries the eggs
in the
same way

A large and familiar spider, thanks to the female's habit of building a protective tent web over some vegetation, in which the eggs or young live, and sitting on it to guard them. At first, she carries the egg sac around with her, then just before the young are about to hatch, she builds the tent. They are most frequently found in woodland clearings, rough pastures, scrub, and anywhere that there is suitable vegetation and abundant insects. Very common and widespread throughout Britain and Europe.

female Nursery Web Spider
carrying egg sac

SPIDERS, ARANEAE

J	F	M	A	M	J
J	A	S	O	N	D

Raft Spider
Dolomedes fimbriatus

ID FACT FILE

SIZE:
Body length
Females up to
22 mm, males
much smaller

DESCRIPTION:
A dark brown
spider, with
white or
yellowish stripes
down both sides
of the carapace
and abdomen –
a distinctive
combination

FOOD:
Insects,
tadpoles, even
small fish
occasionally

LOOKALIKES:
The Great Raft
Spider *D.
plantarius* is
actually no
larger, but differs
in minor details
and is usually
paler. Rare and
protected in
Britain,
uncommon
elsewhere

A large and impressive spider with distinctive
markings and habits. They live in damp places
close to water, and hunt by sitting close to the
water with the front legs resting on the surface
to detect movements made by potential prey.
They will run out across the water, or become
submerged, and catch prey simply by chasing
it. They can remain submerged for up to an
hour if trying to escape predation. They are
widespread, though never common, in marshy
and boggy places, usually with open water,
throughout though rarest in the north.

SPIDERS, ARANEAE

Agelena labrynthica

ID FACT FILE

SIZE:
Body length up to 12 mm

DESCRIPTION:
A brownish spider, with a red-brown carapace that has paler bands; the most distinctive feature is the pale 'herring bone' pattern on the brown abdomen

FOOD:
Insects

LOOKALIKES:
A. gracilens is similar but generally darker; not in UK

This spider builds a large, untidy, sheet web, with a tubular retreat at one corner, in which the female sits and waits. The net is not sticky, but insects become entangled, and the spider rushes out from the tunnel to bite the unfortunate victim, which is then taken back to the tunnel to be eaten at leisure. They are very sensitive to vibrations, and tend to retreat to their tunnel if they hear anyone coming. It is widespread and common in rough habitats, especially on heathland with gorse, throughout England and Wales, and most of Europe.

SPIDERS, ARANEAE

J F M A M J
J A S O N D

females all year;
males in autumn

ID FACT FILE

SIZE:
Body length up to
18 mm

DESCRIPTION:
Generally dark
brown with long
brown legs. The
carapace is
brown with two
rows of darker
radiating marks
and a pale edge;
the abdomen
has a central
pale line with
regular 'commas'
extending out
from it

FOOD:
Various insects

LOOKALIKES:
There are several
similar species,
hard to identify
without detailed
examination

A House Spider
Tegenaria gigantea (T. duellica)

A very large and active spider, with long legs,
that has a habit of running about rapidly in
houses, causing consternation among the
inhabitants. These individuals are usually males
in late summer, looking for females, and it is at
this time that they often become trapped in
baths. However, like most European spiders,
they are harmless. They are most frequent in
houses and outhouses, though also occur in
banks, under logs and in other protected
situations in the milder parts of the region. It is
common and widespread throughout.

SPIDERS, ARANEAE

| J | F | M | A | M | J |
| J | A | S | O | N | D |

Garden Spider
Araneus diadematus

ID FACT FILE

SIZE:
Body length
10–13 mm

DESCRIPTION:
Predominantly
brown or orange-
brown, with a
pattern of white
dots in an
approximate
cross on the
abdomen. The
legs are bristly
and banded
brown and white

FOOD:
Insects

LOOKALIKES:
Other orb-web
spiders are rather
similar, including
A. quadratus
(p.237), but none
has the white
cross

Garden spiders are the best known of all the
orb-web spiders, and most people with a
garden will have come across them. The orb-
web spiders build large roughly circular webs
with radiating spokes, and sit at the centre
waiting for prey. When an insect flies or jumps
into the web, the spider rushes to it and quickly
wraps it in silk. If disturbed, the spider retreats
to a hidden area at the edge of the web. They
are very common and widespread in gardens,
woods and scrub, throughout Britain and
Europe, becoming most noticeable in autumn.

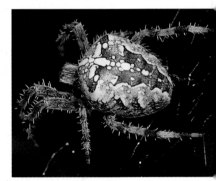

Garden Spider's
orb web

J	F	M	A	M	J
J	A	S	O	N	D

Araneus quadratus

ID FACT FILE

SIZE:
Body length up to 20 mm. Males are smaller

DESCRIPTION:
A large, almost spherical-bodied spider when mature. The abdomen varies from almost green to brown or red, but usually has four round spots in addition to other pale marks

FOOD:
Insects

LOOKALIKES:
None

Although less familiar than the Garden Spider, and not regularly seen in gardens, this spider is even larger and very distinctively marked. The females spend more time in a substantial retreat than in the centre of the web, so they are easily overlooked, though they quickly emerge if an insect becomes trapped in the web. They are moderately common in rough vegetated areas such as wet heaths, ungrazed grassland and scrub. It is widespread throughout Britain and much of Europe except the extremes.

SPIDERS, ARANEAE

J	F	M	A	M	J
J	A	S	O	N	D

Araniella cucurbitina

ID FACT FILE

SIZE:
Body length
about 6 mm

DESCRIPTION:
The legs and
carapace are
brownish, while
the abdomen is
swollen and
bright green,
edged paler;
there is usually a
small red spot

FOOD:
Small insects

LOOKALIKES:
A. opisthographa
is almost
identical apart
from minor
differences in
structure

This little spider is closely related to the orb-web spiders, and it spins a web that can be like a small orb web, though it is often quite eccentric and haphazard in construction. Although small in size, its bright colours make it quite conspicuous in the field. It occurs in a wide variety of habitats, wherever there are bushes and small trees, usually occurring at a height of 1–2 m. It is common and widespread throughout Britain and Europe except the coldest or driest areas.

| J | F | M | A | M | J |
| J | A | S | O | N | D |

Argiope bruenichii

ID FACT FILE

SIZE:
Body length
15 mm (males
much smaller,
4–5 mm)

DESCRIPTION:
The carapace is
pale brownish
with grey hairs;
the oval
abdomen is
horizontally and
irregularly striped
black, yellow and
white. The legs
are banded
yellow and black

FOOD:
Insects

LOOKALIKES:
None

A dramatic and very distinctive spider, sometimes known as the wasp spider thanks to its black and yellow banding. It is primarily a south European species, though it extends northwards to Germany and Holland, and has recently been appearing in new sites in southern Britain. The webs of *Argiope* are orb-like, placed low down in vegetation, but usually have an additional zig-zag strengthened area, known as the stabilimentum. It occurs in a variety of rough habitats such as heathland and grassy scrub.

Argiope web with stabilimentum

SPIDERS, ARANEAE

J	F	M	A	M	J
J	A	S	O	N	D

Argiope lobata

ID FACT FILE

SIZE:
Body length up to
25 mm

DESCRIPTION:
A predominantly
black and white
or brown and
white spider. The
abdomen is
flattened and
strongly lobed
around the edge,
variably marked
with bands of
black or brown.

FOOD:
Insects up to and
including
dragonflies

LOOKALIKES:
None

This is one of Europe's most distinctive and
impressive spiders, with bold markings and a
strongly lobed abdomen, more reminiscent of
some tropical spiders. It builds a web similar to
that of *A. bruenichii* (p.239) amongst shrubs or
rough grass and herbs, up to 2 m above ground
level. The eggs are enclosed in an urn-shaped
cocoon. It is a southern species, found only
close to the Mediterranean, and eastwards
right across southern Asia. Favoured habitats
include sand-dunes, garrigue and scrub.

A. lobata with Lesser Emperor Dragonfly

Harvestman
Phalangium opilio

ID FACT FILE

SIZE:
Body length
5–6 mm,
dwarfed by leg
length

DESCRIPTION:
A rather
undistinguished
creature, greyish
above with paler
markings, and
white below. The
males are more
distinctive, as
they have long
forward-curved
jaws

FOOD:
Other
invertebrates,
and carrion

LOOKALIKES:
*Leiobunum
rotundum* (p.242)
is rather similar

Harvestmen are a small group, resembling spiders, but with a one-piece body. Most have long thin legs. This is one of the commonest of harvestmen, occurring almost everywhere, and frequently seen because it is less nocturnal than most other harvestmen. It has long legs and seems to float over vegetation and other surfaces with ease. The females have long ovipositors, with which the eggs are laid deep into the ground. They occur in a wide variety of habitats including gardens, woodland clearings, scrub and rough grassland. It is widespread throughout Britain and most of Europe.

A Harvestman
Leiobunum rotundum

ID FACT FILE

SIZE:
Body length
about 6 mm

DESCRIPTION:
The body is
brownish-grey
and
unremarkable.
Unlike
Phalangium
(p.241), the
male's jaws are
not greatly
enlarged. The
most distinctive
feature is the
very long thin
legs

FOOD:
Various insects
and other
invertebrates;
some carrion

LOOKALIKES:
*See Phalangium
opilio* (p.241)

This harvestman has a small globular body and
extremely long thin legs, making a curious
contrast. The long legs are very flexible,
allowing it to run easily through uneven
vegetation at a considerable speed. Unlike the
previous species, this one is mainly nocturnal,
coming out from its tree-trunk hideaway at
dusk to feed amongst low-growing vegetation,
then returning to the tree before dawn. It is
common in woods, scrub and older gardens,
throughout most of Britain and Europe.

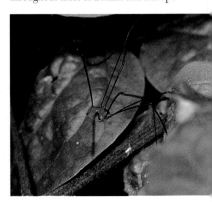

J	F	M	A	M	J
J	A	S	O	N	D

A Centipede
Lithobius forficatus

ID FACT FILE

SIZE:
Body length
3–4 cm

DESCRIPTION:
A long, thin,
flattened animal,
reddish brown in
colour, with 15
pairs of legs at
one pair per
segment. It has
long antennae

FOOD:
Various
invertebrates

LOOKALIKES:
L. variegatus is
very similar, with
minor
differences; it
is mainly a
woodland species

Centipedes are mobile predatory arthropods,
with just one leg per segment, compared to the
two per segment of millipedes. This is one of the
commonest species, being found in a wide
variety of habitats and quite often coming into
houses and sheds at night in search of prey. It is
an aggressive predator, hunting down almost any
suitable-sized creature including slugs, and even
other centipedes. They are nocturnal, hiding
under logs and stones by day. It is common and
widespread except in the driest or coldest areas.

a section of centipede body
showing one leg per segment

J	F	M	A	M	J
J	A	S	O	N	D

A Centipede
Scutigera coleoptrata

ID FACT FILE

SIZE:
Body length
25–35 mm

DESCRIPTION:
Greyish brown in
colour; its most
distinctive
feature is the 15
pairs of very long
legs which
spread widely,
making the
animal appear
almost square
overall. It also
has long
antennae

FOOD:
Various
invertebrates

LOOKALIKES:
None

This is a particularly distinctive species of
centipede, with very long legs and antennae. It
is more likely to be seen in daylight than most
centipedes, as it hunts actively at all times, and
not infrequently comes into houses. It is very
fast-moving, and has excellent eyesight. Its
main habitats are in and around buildings, or
on cliffs and walls. It is widespread in Europe
except the far north, but very rare and southern
in Britain, mainly in the Channel Islands.

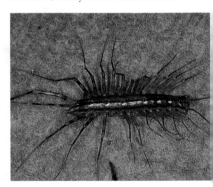

WOODLICE, ISOPODA

J	F	M	A	M	J
J	A	S	O	N	D

Woodlouse

Oniscus asellus

ID FACT FILE

Size:
Body length
16–19 mm

Description:
A greyish-brown,
flattened animal,
paler around the
edges. There is
usually a pale
line of dots down
the centre

Food:
All sorts of
scavenged
material

Lookalikes:
There are several
similar species

This is one of the largest and commonest of woodlice, of which there are a number of similar species. Woodlice suffer from not being able to prevent themselves drying out, so they spend most of their time out of the sunlight, hidden under stones or logs, and foraging at night. The females carry the eggs or young in a special pouch under the body, keeping them humid. This species is common in a variety of habitats wherever suitable sheltered humid conditions occur. It is widespread throughout Britain and much of Europe.

WOODLICE, ISOPODA

J F M A M J
J A S O N D

Sea Slater
Ligia oceanica

ID FACT FILE

SIZE:
Body length up to 30 mm

DESCRIPTION:
A large flattened greyish or grey-brown woodlouse-shaped animal, with numerous visible legs and long antennae and appendages

FOOD:
Scavengers and plant feeders

LOOKALIKES:
Nothing comparable in north Europe, though there are rather similar Mediterranean species

This distinctive animal is like a very large woodlouse. It is confined to the intertidal area of rocky seashores, living on algae and other plant material. They are mainly nocturnal, but quite often venture out in the daytime especially if disturbed in their hiding place. They live for up to three years, breeding in their third year. It is common and widespread along rocky shores, even where quite exposed, throughout western Europe and parts of the Mediterranean.

| J | F | M | A | M | J |
| J | A | S | O | N | D |

A Pill Millipede
Glomeris marginata

ID FACT FILE

SIZE:
Body length
13–15 mm

DESCRIPTION:
A greyish-brown
animal, with
about eleven
tightly fitting
calcareous
plates down its
back, with
numerous short
legs hidden
beneath this

FOOD:
Plant material of
various sorts

LOOKALIKES:
There are closely
related species.
Also, the Pill
Woodlouse
*Armadillidium
vulgare* is very
similar, but has
fewer legs and a
series of small
plates at the rear
end. It is
common

The pill-millipedes are an intriguing little group
of invertebrates, rather resembling woodlice but
closer to millipedes. The common name refers
to its habit of rolling into a tight ball if
threatened, to protect its soft underparts. It is
able to withstand desiccation better than other
millipedes, and can be found in a wider range of
situations including woodland, chalk grassland
and gardens. They are quite long-lived, lasting
for 6–7 years, becoming mature when they are
about three. It is common and widespread
throughout Britain and most of Europe.

pill woodlouse

pill millipede

TICKS AND MITES, ACARI

J	F	M	A	M	J
J	A	S	O	N	D

Sheep Tick

Ixodes ricinus

ID FACT FILE

SIZE:
Body length
3–4 mm

DESCRIPTION:
A greyish-brown
oval creature,
with six legs as a
young larva, or
eight reddish
legs when
mature. When
fully fed, they
resemble a small
reddish bean

FOOD:
Mammalian
blood

LOOKALIKES:
There are several
rather similar
species

Also known as the Castor Bean, because of its
shape when fully swollen, this is the
commonest and most economically significant
of the ticks. They have a strange life-cycle,
taking about three years and involving high
mortality. The young larva is six-legged, and it
must find a mammalian host to take blood,
after which it moults into an eight-legged
nymph. The following year, this has to find
another mammal before it can become mature.
The female adults then feed again before
mating and laying eggs. They carry various
diseases, and can bite man and dogs. They are
widespread and common almost throughout.

Velvet Mite
Eutrombidium rostratus

J	F	M	A	M	J
J	A	S	O	N	D

ID FACT FILE

SIZE:
Body length
2–3 mm

DESCRIPTION:
Bright red, soft,
slightly pear-
shaped little
creatures, with
eight legs

FOOD:
Scavengers and
carnivores,
mainly on insect
eggs

LOOKALIKES:
Red Spider Mite
Panonychus ulmi
is darker, and
narrowest at the
head end. On
fruit trees

These are attractive and harmless little creatures, with no significant economic importance (not to be confused with Red Spider Mite). The larvae attach themselves to a suitable host such as a grasshopper, and feed for a few days; they drop off and burrow, eventually emerging as free-living creatures. These are the stage most often noticed as the nymphs or adults roam over soil and paths in search of food. They are widespread and often very abundant in a wide variety of habitats especially where there is some bare ground.

INDEX

Main entries in the text appear with a **bold** page reference.

OTHER COLLINS WILD GUIDES

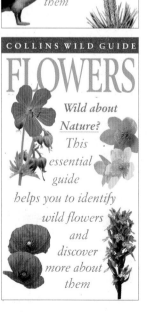
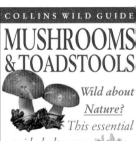